# Green Line 2 G9

## Fit für Tests und Klassenarbeite



von
Pauline Ashworth
Niamh Humphreys

herausgegeben von
Harald Weisshaar

Ernst Klett Verlag
Stuttgart · Leipzig

Hallo! In diesem Heft haben wir für dich passend zu deinem Green Line-Englischbuch Tests und Klassenarbeiten zusammengestellt, damit du dich gut auf diese vorbereiten kannst. Du lernst auch, dir die Zeit zur Bearbeitung der Aufgaben einzuteilen – pro Test hast du maximal 25 Minuten Zeit, pro Klassenarbeit maximal 45 Minuten.
Während die Tests die neuen Wörter und die Grammatik abfragen, musst du in den Klassenarbeiten Lesetexte, Hörtexte und manchmal auch Filme verstehen können, Texte selbst schreiben oder als Sprachmittler tätig werden.
Hinten im Heft findest du auf den Seiten 65 bis 70 Aufgaben, die dir helfen, dich auf mündliche Leistungskontrollen vorzubereiten.

Auf den Seiten 4 bis 7 geben dir Tony und Lou Tipps zu allen Kompetenzen. Sie helfen dir beim Lernen und der Vorbereitung auf Tests und Klassenarbeiten. Außerdem findest du auf den Seiten 8 und 9 kurze Erklärungen zu den wichtigsten Aufgabenformaten – diese werden dir immer wieder begegnen. Schau sie dir deshalb sorgfältig an!

Nach der Überschrift *Test* bzw. *Class test* zeigt dir der Verweis an, wann du den Test bzw. die Klassenarbeit am besten machst, z. B. → after Station 1 bedeutet, dass du den Test bearbeiten sollst, nachdem ihr Station 1 der betreffenden Unit im Unterricht behandelt habt.

Die Hörtexte und Filme findest du auf der CD-ROM, die diesem Heft beiliegt. Die Ziffer neben dem CD-Symbol gibt die jeweilige Tracknummer an.

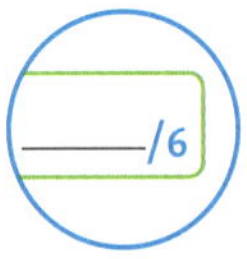


Neben jeder Aufgabe steht ein Kästchen, in das du die erreichte Punktzahl einträgst. Am Ende eines Tests bzw. einer Klassenarbeit zählst du deine Punkte zusammen.
In den Tests erhältst du einen Punkt pro richtige Lösung.
In den Klassenarbeiten bekommst du einen Punkt für jede richtige Antwort bei *Reading*, *Listening* und *Viewing*. Wenn du bei *Writing* und *Mediation* ganze Sätze schreibst, gibt es pro Satz zwei Punkte – einen Punkt für den Inhalt und einen für die sprachliche Richtigkeit.

Im beiliegenden Lösungsheft findest du alle Lösungen und Lösungsvorschläge sowie Checklisten zur Auswertung deiner Ergebnisse. Bei den Checklisten findest du auch Hinweise auf weitere Übungen zum Wiederholen und Festigen. Sie helfen dir deine Schwächen zu beheben.
Dieses Symbol bedeutet, dass du die Transkripte zu den Hörtexten und Filmen auf der CD-ROM findest.
Übrigens ist das Lösungsheft auch auf der CD-ROM für den Fall, dass es einmal verloren gehen sollte.

# Inhalt

Die folgenden Tipps und Strategien können dir dabei helfen, dich auf Tests und Klassenarbeiten vorzubereiten und ein gutes Ergebnis zu erzielen.

## Allgemeine Tipps und Strategien

Suche dir einen festen Arbeitsplatz (z. B. der Schreibtisch in deinem Zimmer). Achte darauf, dass du dort genügend Licht und Ruhe hast. Außerdem brauchst du dein Englischbuch, verschiedenfarbige Stifte und Papier für Notizen.

Fange rechtzeitig damit an zu lernen, also nicht erst am Tag vor einem Test bzw. der nächsten Klassenarbeit. So bleibt dir ausreichend Zeit, um den Lernstoff nochmals zu wiederholen, wenn du beim Üben feststellst, dass du noch nicht alles kannst.

Plane genügend Zeit ein, um einen Test (ca. 25 Minuten) oder eine Klassenarbeit (ca. 45 Minuten) zu bearbeiten. Teile dir die Zeit gut ein – schaue ab und zu auf die Uhr, damit du weißt, wie viel Zeit du noch hast.
Sollte dir eine Aufgabe Probleme bereiten, mache am besten mit der nächsten weiter, damit du nicht zu viel Zeit verlierst. Gehe später noch einmal zu der übersprungenen Aufgabe zurück und versuche erneut sie zu lösen.

Lies dir die Arbeitsanweisungen und Aufgabenstellungen / Fragen immer ganz genau durch, damit du weißt, was zu tun ist.

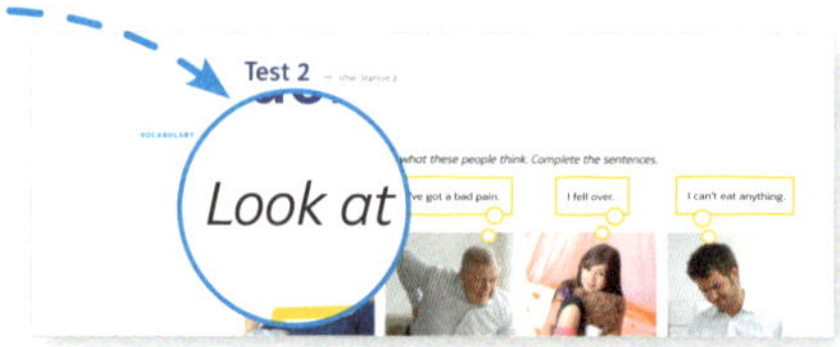


### Vocabulary

- Lerne die neuen Vokabeln in deinem Englischbuch stets sorgfältig! Sie werden dir immer wieder begegnen: in Hörverstehenstexten, in Lesetexten und bei Sprachmittlungsaufgaben. Auch beim Schreiben von Texten wirst du sie brauchen.
- In deinem Englischbuch findest du auf den Seiten 128–129 viele Tipps, die dir das Lernen von neuen Wörtern erleichtern, z. B. wie du ein Vokabelheft oder eine Vokabelkartei anlegst und wie du dir neue Wörter erschließen und merken kannst.

### Language

- Lies dir die Grammatikregeln in deinem Englischbuch ab Seite 140 sorgfältig durch und versuche sie dir einzuprägen, z. B. indem du sie auf Karteikarten oder ein Poster schreibst. Das Beherrschen der Grammatik hilft dir, Fehler bei Schreib-, Sprech- und Sprachmittlungsaufgaben zu vermeiden.
- Manchmal gibt es in den Aufgaben Signalwörter (z. B. bei den Zeitformen), die dir helfen, die richtige Lösung zu finden.

## Listening

Beim Hörverstehen gibt es unterschiedliche Techniken:
- *Listening for gist*, d.h. du erkennst die wichtigsten Informationen und fasst sie zusammen.
- *Listening for detail*, d.h. du entnimmst einem Hörtext bestimmte Einzelheiten.

In Tests und Klassenarbeiten hörst du den Hörtext meistens zweimal:

**Vor dem ersten Hören**
- Lies dir die Überschrift, die Arbeitsanweisung und alle Aufgaben / Fragen genau durch.
- Falls es ein Bild zur Aufgabe gibt, schaue es dir an und versuche auf den Inhalt des Hörtextes zu schließen. Überlege, um welche Textsorte es sich handeln könnte.

**Beim ersten Hören**
- Beantworte alle Aufgaben / Fragen, deren Lösung du schon weißt.
- Du kannst dir auch unter den folgenden Überschriften Notizen machen:
  *Who …?* *What …?* *Where …?* *When …?*

**Beim zweiten Hören**
- Achte jetzt gezielt auf die Details und die Inhalte, die dir noch unklar sind. Berücksichtige dabei auch die Geräusche sowie die Stimme und den Tonfall des Sprechers. Beantworte dann die restlichen Aufgaben / Fragen.
- Achtung: Manchmal kommen die Informationen, die du zur Bearbeitung einer Aufgabe benötigst, im Hörtext in einer anderen Reihenfolge vor.
- Lies dir nach dem zweiten Hören deine Antworten noch einmal durch und überprüfe sie auf inhaltliche und sprachliche Fehler.

## Viewing

- Lies dir die Arbeitsanweisung und die Aufgaben / Fragen genau durch, bevor du dir den Film ansiehst, damit du weißt, worauf du achten musst.
- Schau dir den Film am besten zweimal an – so kannst du dich beim ersten Durchgang an die Stimmen und die Sprechgeschwindigkeit gewöhnen und erfährst schon einmal grob worum es geht: Wer macht was, wann und wo?
- Um der Handlung folgen zu können, musst du nicht jedes Wort verstehen. Die Mimik und Gestik der Schauspieler können dir ebenso helfen wie ihr Tonfall und die Lautstärke, in der sie reden. Achte außerdem auf den Handlungsort (z.B. Landschaften, Gebäude, Gegenstände) und die Kameraeinstellungen (z.B. Nahaufnahmen), denn sie können dir helfen den Inhalt besser zu verstehen. Als Hilfestellung sind die Filme zudem mit englischen Untertiteln versehen, die du ein- oder ausblenden kannst.
- Manche Aufgaben / Fragen kannst du vielleicht schon lösen, während du den Film anschaust. Halte dich aber beim Schauen nicht zu sehr mit den Aufgaben auf, sonst könntest du wichtige Informationen verpassen!

## Reading

Es gibt zwei Schnelllesetechniken, die du anwenden kannst:
- *Skimming*, d.h. du überfliegst den Text, um die wichtigsten Informationen zu erfassen.
- *Scanning*, d.h. du suchst den Text nach Details ab und konzentrierst dich auf bestimmte Stichwörter und Textstellen.

Lies dir jeden Text mindestens zweimal durch:

**Vor dem ersten Lesen**
- Lies die Überschrift und falls es ein Bild gibt, schau es dir an. Überlege um welche Textsorte es sich handeln könnte (z.B. eine Website, eine Geschichte, eine E-Mail).

**Beim ersten Lesen**
- Denke daran, dass das erste Lesen darauf abzielt zu erkennen, worum es in dem Text geht. Dazu brauchst du nicht jedes Wort zu verstehen.
- Du kannst dir unter den folgenden Überschriften Notizen machen: *Who …? What …? When …? Where …?*

**Nach dem ersten Lesen**
- Wenn du Einzelheiten nicht verstanden hast, ist das kein Grund zur Sorge – sieh dir erst einmal die Arbeitsanweisung und die Aufgaben / Fragen genau an.

**Beim zweiten Lesen**
- Suche jetzt im Text gezielt nach den Informationen, die du zur Lösung der Aufgaben / Fragen benötigst. Markiere wichtige Textstellen und mache dir Notizen.
- Frage dich bei unbekannten Wörtern, ob du einen Teil des Wortes oder ein Wort aus der gleichen Wortfamilie schon kennst. Gibt es ein ähnliches Wort im Deutschen oder in anderen Sprachen? Kannst du die Bedeutung aus dem Zusammenhang erschließen?
- Achte darauf, wie und in welcher Zeitform die Fragen gestellt sind und beantworte sie entsprechend (z.B. *Where did they go for their summer holidays?* → *They went to …* .).
- Überprüfe zum Schluss deine Lösungen noch einmal.

## Writing

- Lies dir die Arbeitsanweisung und die Aufgaben / Fragen genau durch.
- Überlege für wen der Text bestimmt ist und welchen Zweck er erfüllen soll.
- Denke darüber nach, was du schreiben willst und mache dir Notizen. Bringe deine Notizen dann in eine logische Reihenfolge.
- Achte darauf, dass verschiedene Textsorten bestimmte Merkmale haben. Schau dir dazu die Tabelle in deinem Buch auf Seite 132 genau an.
- Erstelle vor dem Schreiben eine Gliederung und notiere in Stichwörtern, was in der Einleitung, im Hauptteil und am Schluss stehen soll.
- Beim Schreiben sind nicht nur deine eigenen Ideen gefragt, sondern auch dein sprachlicher Ausdruck. Achte deshalb auf den Inhalt, die Rechtschreibung, die Grammatik, die Wortstellung und den Satzbau.
- Versuche deinen Text interessant und abwechslungsreich zu schreiben. Benutze dazu Adjektive (z.B. *confident, nervous*), Adverbien (z.B. *slowly, well*), Bindewörter (z.B. *and, so*), Häufigkeitsadverbien (z.B. *always, never*), Zeitangaben (z.B. *tomorrow, yesterday*) und Satzgefüge aus Haupt- und Nebensätzen (z.B. *I was really happy because my best friend Ben sat next to me on the coach trip to London*).
- Denke bei Briefen und E-Mails daran, eine passende Anrede (z.B. *Dear …*) und Verabschiedung (z.B. *Yours / Love / Best wishes*) zu verwenden.
- Lies deinen Text zum Schluss noch einmal genau durch und überprüfe ihn auf Fehler.

## Mediation

- Sätze und Texte kannst du oftmals nicht wortwörtlich übersetzen – und das sollst du auch nicht, denn bei der Sprachmittlung geht es darum, die wichtigsten Informationen in die andere Sprache zu übertragen.
- Achte darauf, für wen die Informationen bestimmt sind und was die Person vielleicht schon weiß.
- Überlege, wozu die Person die Informationen benötigt und gebe nur die Informationen weiter, die für sie in der betreffenden Situation wichtig sind. Manchmal ist es aber auch notwendig, bestimmte Dinge zusätzlich zu erklären.
- Du kannst einen längeren Satz einfacher in die andere Sprache übertragen, indem du ihn in mehrere kurze Sätze unterteilst, z. B. indem du „Frage ihn, was man dort unternehmen kann und wie man am besten dorthin kommt." mit *"What can you do there? And how can you get there?"* wiedergibst.
- Wenn du ein Wort nicht weißt oder es dir nicht einfällt, versuche es zu umschreiben, z. B. indem du „Jugendliche" mit *"young people"* wiedergibst.
- Achte darauf, dass du manchmal die Perspektive und die Satzform ändern musst, z. B. aus „Frage ihn, ob er schon beim Arzt war." wird dann *"Have you been to the doctor's yet?"*
- Denke an die Unterschiede zwischen dem Englischen und Deutschen, z. B. in der Wortstellung, bei den Präpositionen und in der Verwendung verschiedener Zeitformen:
  → *Olivia* ***often runs*** *in the park.* (*simple present*, weil sie dies regelmäßig tut; das Häufigkeitsadverb steht vor dem Verb)
  → *She* ***is running*** *in the park* ***now****.* (*present progressive*, weil sie es jetzt gerade tut; die Zeitangabe steht am Satzende)

## Speaking

- Lies dir die Arbeitsanweisung und Aufgabenstellung genau durch.
- Überlege dir, um was für eine Gesprächssituation es sich handelt.
- Mache dir stichpunktartige Notizen. Schreibe keine ganzen Sätze!
- Sprich langsam und deutlich, sodass man dich gut verstehen kann.
- Denke daran Höflichkeitsformen zu verwenden und auf deinen Gesprächspartner einzugehen.
- Wenn du sprichst, ist es normal, dass Pausen, unvollständige Sätze, Wiederholungen und Füllwörter vorkommen, z. B. ***Well****, I don't really know.* ***Er****, I'm not sure about that.*
- Beantworte Fragen nicht nur mit *Yes.* oder *No.*, sondern mit Kurzantworten oder ganzen Sätzen, wie z. B. *Yes, I do. / No, I don't.* oder *Yes, she loves cooking. / No, he isn't at home.*
- Frage nach, wenn du etwas nicht verstanden hast, z. B. *Sorry. Can you say that again, please?* oder *Excuse me. What does that mean?*
- Wenn du zu Hause übst, kannst du dich selbst aufnehmen und dich so überprüfen.
- Du kannst dich natürlich auch mit einem Freund oder einer Freundin verabreden oder mit jemandem üben, der etwas Englisch kann (z. B. älteren Geschwistern, deiner Mutter oder deinem Vater).

# Wichtige Aufgabenformate

## A Listening / Reading / Viewing

1. ***Single choice:*** *Tick ✔ the correct answer.*
Hier werden Fragen zum Textverständnis gestellt, für die es meist drei oder vier Antwortmöglichkeiten gibt. Deine Aufgabe ist es, dich für eine richtige Antwort zu entscheiden und ein Häkchen in das dazugehörige Kästchen zu setzen.

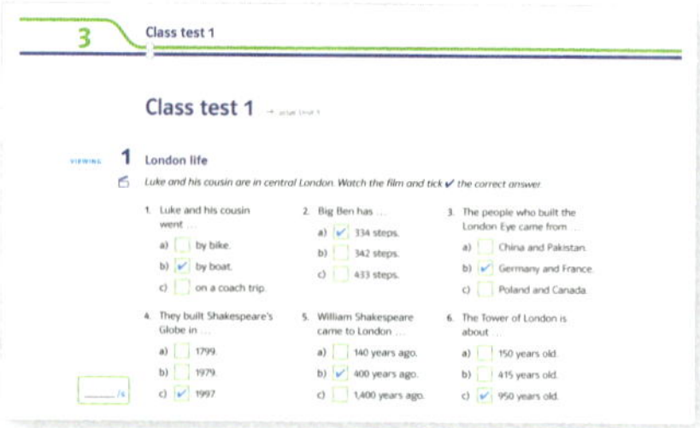

3 Class test 1

Class test 1

VIEWING 1 London life

*Luke and his cousin are in central London. Watch the film and tick ✔ the correct answer.*

1. Luke and his cousin went …
   a) by bike.
   b) ✔ by boat.
   c) on a coach trip.
2. Big Ben has …
   a) ✔ 334 steps.
   b) 342 steps.
   c) 433 steps.
3. The people who built the London Eye came from …
   a) China and Pakistan.
   b) ✔ Germany and France.
   c) Poland and Canada.
4. They built Shakespeare's Globe in …
   a) 1799.
   b) 1979.
   c) ✔ 1997.
5. William Shakespeare came to London …
   a) 140 years ago.
   b) ✔ 400 years ago.
   c) 1,400 years ago.
6. The Tower of London is about …
   a) 150 years old.
   b) 415 years old.
   c) ✔ 950 years old.

___ /6

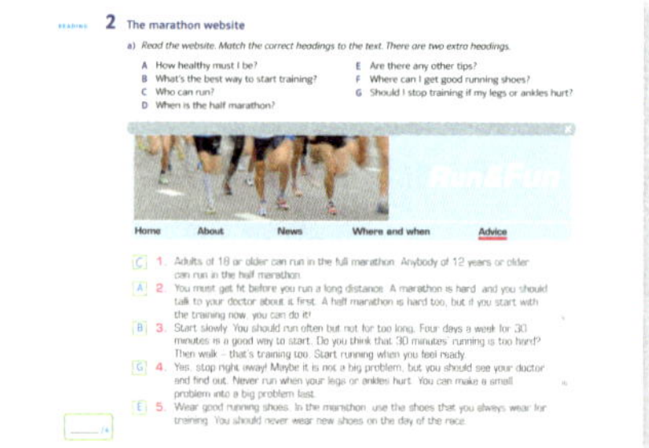

READING 2 The marathon website

a) *Read the website. Match the correct headings to the text. There are two extra headings.*

A How healthy must I be?
B What's the best way to start training?
C Who can run?
D When is the half marathon?
E Are there any other tips?
F Where can I get good running shoes?
G Should I stop training if my legs or ankles hurt?

Home About News Where and when Advice

C 1. Adults of 18 or older can run in the full marathon. Anybody of 12 years or older can run in the half marathon.
A 2. You must get fit before you run a long distance. A marathon is hard, and you should talk to your doctor about it first. A half marathon is hard too, but if you start with the training now, you can do it!
B 3. Start slowly. You should run often but not for too long. Four days a week for 30 minutes is a good way to start. Do you think that 30 minutes' running is too hard? Then walk – that's training too. Start running when you feel ready.
G 4. Yes, stop right away! Maybe it is not a big problem, but you should see your doctor and find out. Never run when your legs or ankles hurt. You can make a small problem into a big problem fast.
E 5. Wear good running shoes. In the marathon, use the shoes that you always wear for training. You should never wear new shoes on the day of the race.

___ /4

2. ***Multiple matching:*** *Read the texts. Match them with the headings / pictures. (There are two extra headings / pictures.)*
Diese Art von Aufgabe findest du nur bei Lesetexten. Hier sollst du verschiedene Texte oder Textabschnitte entweder Bildern oder Überschriften zuordnen. Es kann sein, dass es mehr Überschriften oder Bilder gibt als du brauchst!

3. ***Sequencing:*** *Put the parts of the story / sentences in the correct order.*
Hier sollst du dir zunächst Textabschnitte oder Sätze durchlesen und diese dann in die richtige Reihenfolge bringen, indem du den richtigen Buchstaben (oder die richtige Zahl) notierst.

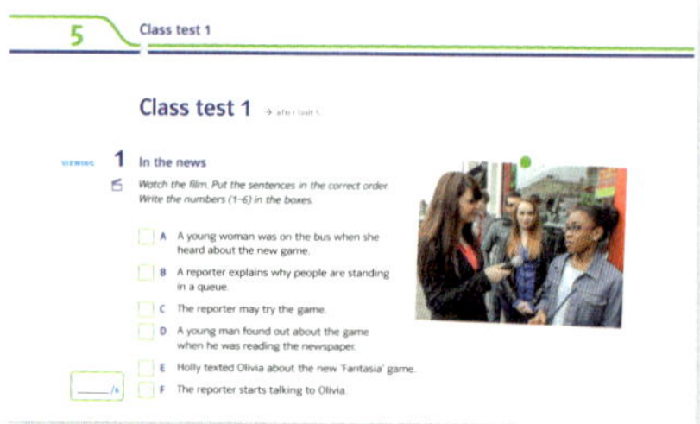

5 Class test 1

Class test 1

VIEWING 1 In the news

*Watch the film. Put the sentences in the correct order. Write the numbers (1–6) in the boxes.*

A A young woman was on the bus when she heard about the new game.
B A reporter explains why people are standing in a queue.
C The reporter may try the game.
D A young man found out about the game when he was reading the newspaper.
E Holly texted Olivia about the new 'Fantasia' game.
F The reporter starts talking to Olivia.

___ /6

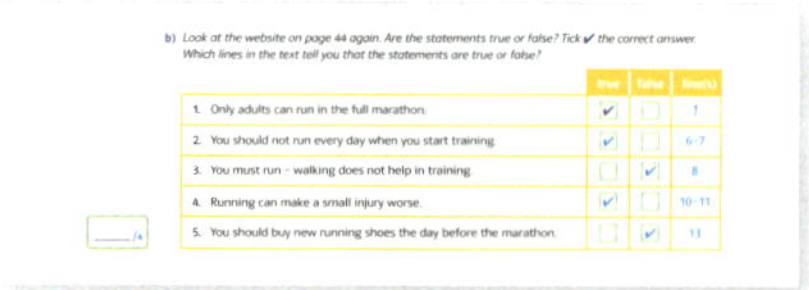

b) *Look at the website on page 44 again. Are the statements true or false? Tick ✔ the correct answer. Which lines in the text tell you that the statements are true or false?*

| | true | false | line(s) |
|---|---|---|---|
| 1. Only adults can run in the full marathon. | ✔ | | 1 |
| 2. You should not run every day when you start training. | ✔ | | 6–7 |
| 3. You must run – walking does not help in training. | | ✔ | 8 |
| 4. Running can make a small injury worse. | ✔ | | 10–11 |
| 5. You should buy new running shoes the day before the marathon. | | ✔ | 13 |

___ /4

4. ***True-false:*** *Are the statements true or false? Tick ✔ the correct answer.*
Diese Aufgaben bestehen aus verschiedenen Aussagen zum Text. Du musst entscheiden, ob sie richtig (*true*) oder falsch (*false*) sind und ein Häkchen in die entsprechende Spalte setzen.
Manchmal gibt es bei *true / false*-Aufgaben zu Lesetexten noch eine zusätzliche Spalte, in der du die Zeilen angeben musst, in denen sich die Information im Lesetext befindet.

5. ***Short open answers:*** *Answer the questions in 1 to 5 words or numbers.*
Hier werden Fragen zum Text gestellt, die du in 1 bis 5 Wörtern oder mit einer Zahl beantworten sollst. Schreibe also keine ganzen Sätze!

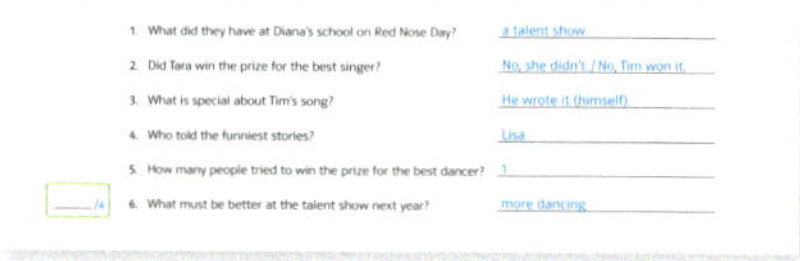

1. What did they have at Diana's school on Red Nose Day? a talent show
2. Did Tara win the prize for the best singer? No, she didn't. / No, Tim won it.
3. What is special about Tim's song? He wrote it (himself).
4. Who told the funniest stories? Lisa
5. How many people tried to win the prize for the best dancer? 1
6. What must be better at the talent show next year? more dancing

___ /6

6. ***Table completion:*** *Complete the table. (Use 1 to 5 words or numbers.)*
Bei diesen Aufgaben liegt eine Tabelle vor, die manchmal schon zum Teil ausgefüllt ist. Während des Hörens oder Lesens füllst du sie aus. Meist solltest du dabei nur 1 bis 5 Wörter oder Zahlen verwenden. Schreibe also keine ganzen Sätze!

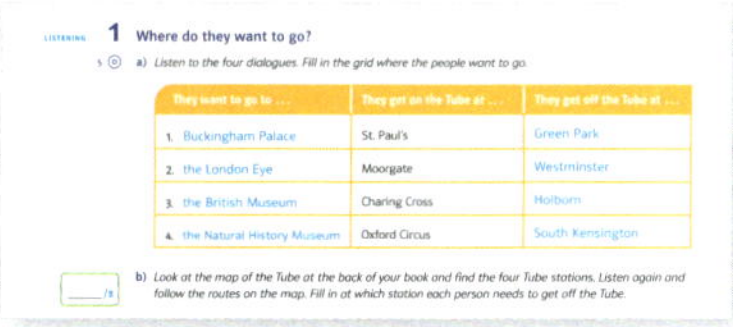
1 Where do they want to go?
a) Listen to the four dialogues. Fill in the grid where the people want to go.

| They want to go to ... | They get on the Tube at ... | They get off the Tube at ... |
| --- | --- | --- |
| 1. Buckingham Palace | St Paul's | Green Park |
| 2. the London Eye | Moorgate | Westminster |
| 3. the British Museum | Charing Cross | Holborn |
| 4. the Natural History Museum | Oxford Circus | South Kensington |

b) Look at the map of the Tube at the back of your book and find the four Tube stations. Listen again and follow the routes on the map. Fill in at which station each person needs to get off the Tube.

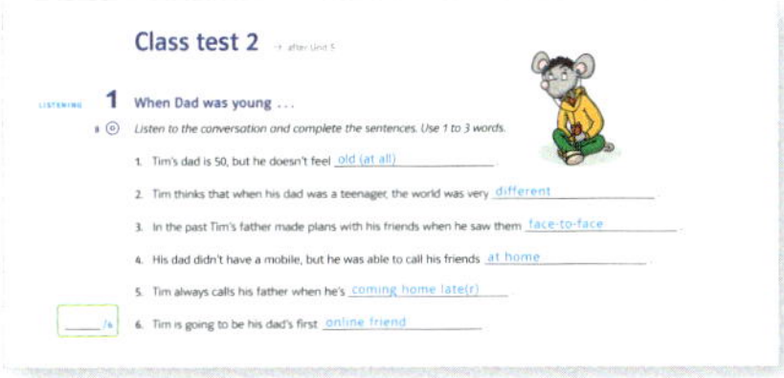
Class test 2
1 When Dad was young ...
Listen to the conversation and complete the sentences. Use 1 to 3 words.
1. Tim's dad is 50, but he doesn't feel old (at all)
2. Tim thinks that when his dad was a teenager, the world was very different
3. In the past Tim's father made plans with his friends when he saw them face-to-face
4. His dad didn't have a mobile, but he was able to call his friends at home
5. Tim always calls his father when he's coming home late(r)
6. Tim is going to be his dad's first online friend

7. ***Sentence completion:*** *Complete the sentences. Use 1 to 3 words.*
Bei diesen Aufgaben werden unvollständige Sätze vorgegeben, die du vervollständigen sollst. Dafür darfst du maximal fünf Wörter benutzen.

8. ***Citing:*** *Copy 1 to 10 words from the text to show that the statements are correct.*
Hier werden Aussagen vorgegeben und du sollst im Text Wörter finden, die die Aussagen belegen. Dazu sollst du 1–10 Wörter aus dem Text aufschreiben.

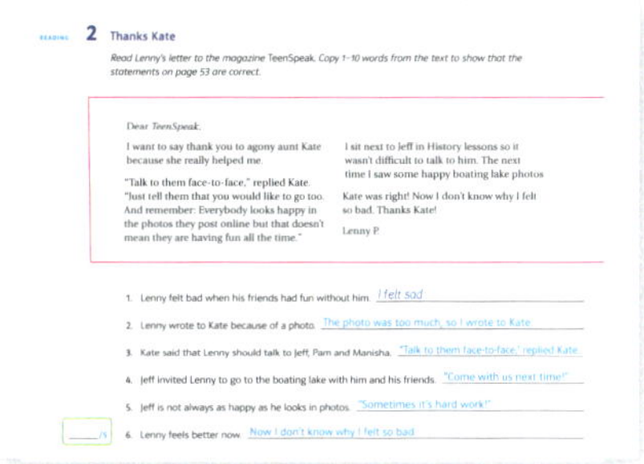
2 Thanks Kate

## B Writing

Bei Schreibaufgaben sollst du einen Text zu einem bestimmten Thema verfassen. Meist ist die Textsorte (z. B. E-Mail, Geschichte) vorgegeben und manchmal auch eine Anzahl der erwarteten Sätze oder Wörter, damit du weißt, wie lang der Text ungefähr werden soll. Oft enthält die Aufgabenstellung Fragen, Stichwörter oder Bilder, die dir beim Schreiben des Textes helfen.

## C Mediation

Bei Sprachmittlungsaufgaben musst du Aussagen sinngemäß vom Deutschen ins Englische oder vom Englischen ins Deutsche übertragen.

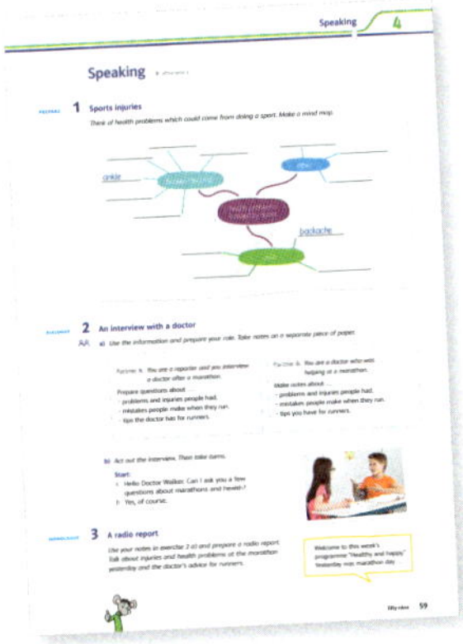

## D Speaking

Wie gut du schon Englisch sprechen kannst, wird in der Regel zusammen mit einem Mitschüler / einer Mitschülerin geprüft. Meist besteht die Prüfung aus drei Teilen:
- Der Lehrer / Die Lehrerin stellt dir Fragen zu einem vorgegebenen Thema.
- Jeder von euch spricht länger am Stück, z. B. über ein Bild, über eure Familie oder über eure Schule (*monologue*).
- Du führst ein Gespräch mit deinem Mitschüler / deiner Mitschülerin (*dialogue*).
Keine Angst! Die meisten Lehrerinnen und Lehrer geben ein paar Minuten Zeit zur Vorbereitung, sodass ihr euch die Aufgabenstellung genau durchlesen, die Vorgaben (z. B. Bilder) anschauen und vielleicht auch ein paar Notizen machen könnt.

# Unit 1 My friends and I

## Test 1 → after Station 1

VOCABULARY

### 1 The noticeboard

*Read the flyer on the noticeboard. Put in the missing words. There are two extra words.*

ago | also | best | enjoy | month✓ | raise | sale | think of

Next month ______ it's that time again – time to ______ money for children in our town. But what can we do? One year ______ we had a great cake ______. Now we need a new activity. Can you ______ a new idea? The ______ suggestion wins a prize! Write your ideas and your name here:

| Name | Year | Idea |
|---|---|---|
| | | |
| | | |
| | | |

____ /5

VOCABULARY

### 2 The school sale

*Look at the picture. Label the things and complete the text on the sign.*

____ /5

LANGUAGE

## 3 Regular simple past forms

*Write the **simple past** form of the verbs.*

1. love loved
2. start ______
3. clap ______
4. plan ______
5. try ______
6. watch ______

Watch the spelling of a verb before you add the **simple past** ending.

____/5

LANGUAGE

## 4 The street show

*Complete the dialogue with the verbs in the **simple past**. There are regular and irregular verbs.*

Luke: We had (have) so much fun yesterday.

Dave: Why?

Luke: We ______ (do) a little comedy show on Church Street in Greenwich.

Dave: That sounds great!

Luke: It was! Olivia ______ (play) the saxophone, Jay and I ______ (dance) and Holly ______ (collect) money.

Dave: But that isn't comedy!

Luke: Oh, it ______ (be) funny. We all ______ (wear) red noses and silly clothes. Sherlock ______ (jump) over boxes and ______ (chase) his tail. People ______ (laugh) a lot!

____/9

____/24

# Test 2 → after Station 2

VOCABULARY

## 1 A job puzzle

*Read the clues and write the words in the puzzle.*

**Across →**
3. He or she works with students in a school.
5. He brings parcels to your house.
6. This person sings in a music band.

**Down ↓**
1. He or she looks after animals like chickens and pigs.
2. You need him or her when your car has a problem.
4. This person takes people to other places in a taxi, bus or coach.

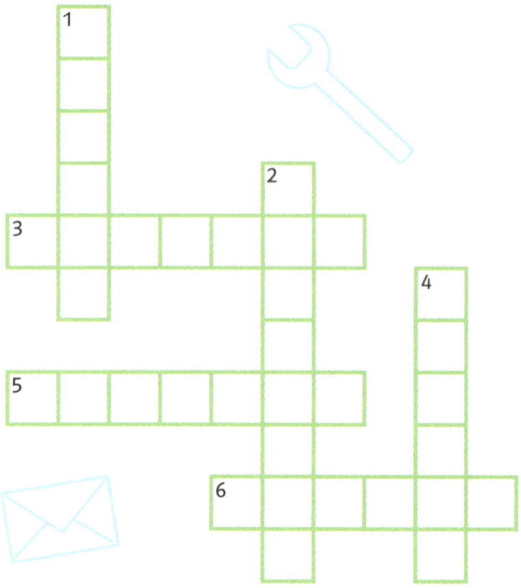


______ /6

VOCABULARY

## 2 Dave's dream

*Put in the missing words. There are three extra words.*

arrest | friendly | missing | month | police | solution | someone | taxi

"In my dream a man called the ________________ and said, "You must find Dave – he's dangerous!" They tried to ________________ me! I jumped into a ________________ and we went away fast. The driver was ________________. I forgot my problems and opened a window, but then ________________ saw me and said, "Hey, there's that dangerous boy!" I was really happy when the dream finished!"

______ /5

LANGUAGE

## 3 Where was Jay?

*Complete the dialogue with the correct simple past form of **do** or **be**.*

1. Was Jay at school yesterday? – No, he wasn't.
2. ________ he stay at home? – No, he didn't.
3. Did he have fun? – Yes, he ____________.
4. ________ he with Holly? – Yes, he was.
5. Were they at the park? – Yes, they ____________!

______ /4

LANGUAGE

## 4 Where did you go?

*Complete the questions with the correct question word and form of the verb.*

how what when where✔ who why

1. Where did you go (you / go) on Sunday? – I went to the swimming pool.
2. ______________________ (you / go) with? – With Dave.
3. ______________________ (you / get) there? – By bus.
4. ______________________ (you / go)? – Because we were bored.
5. ______________________ (you / do) there? – We jumped into the water, of course!
6. ______________________ (you / come) home? – At 6 p.m.

_____ /5

LANGUAGE

## 5 Olivia did, but Luke didn't

*Olivia had a busy day yesterday, but Luke did nothing. Write sentences about Luke.*

Before you write a sentence about Luke underline the verb in the sentence about Olivia.

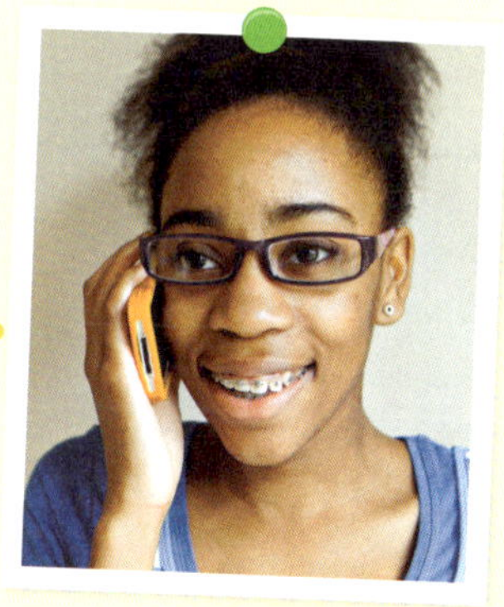

1. Olivia tidied her room. Luke didn't tidy his room.
2. Olivia went cycling. ______________________
3. Olivia made a cake. ______________________
4. Olivia did her homework. ______________________
5. Olivia saw her friends. ______________________
6. Olivia was tired in the evening. ______________________

_____ /5

_____ /25

# Test 3

→ after Station 3

VOCABULARY

## 1 Dave's e-mail

*Read the e-mail from Dave to his friend Tim. Put in the missing words. There are three extra words.*

adventure | Celtic | confident | course | forests | gorge scrambling | mountains | outdoor | tall | Wales | walking

Hi Tim,

Sorry, but I can't meet you on Friday. Our class wants to go to an ______ centre in ______. It's in a national park with ______ and high ______ but … well, you know I'm not really into sports! We can do ______ there. What's that? I hope it's not too hard. I don't feel very ______ about it. ______ in the mountains is OK but climbing? Well, it's all a big ______!

See you next week,

Dave

____/8

LANGUAGE

## 2 The highest mountain

*Look at the pictures and the words. Write the adjectives in the correct form.*

1.

high

higher

the highest

2.

fast

______

______

3.

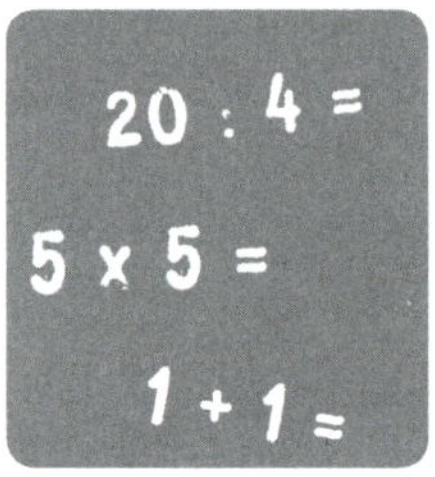


easy

______

______

4.

80 people love this — popular

160 people love this — ______

490 people love this — ______

____/6

LANGUAGE

## 3 Comments on the class trip

*Put in the correct* ***comparative*** *or* ***superlative*** *forms.*

"This year's class trip was ____________________ good than the trip last year. For me gorge scrambling was ____________________ exciting activity. It was also ____________________ hard challenge on the trip."

"Holly, Dave and I fell into the river. The water was ____________________ cold than the sea! I felt cold for the whole day. For me that was ____________________ bad thing about the trip."

____/5

LANGUAGE

## 4 That's not right!

*Correct the information. Write two sentences with different adjectives.*

1. Wales is as big as Germany. small

   No, Wales is not as big as Germany.

   Wales is smaller than Germany.

2. Walking is as hard as climbing. easy

   ______________________________

   ______________________________

3. Dave is as confident as Jay. nervous

   ______________________________

   ______________________________

4. A day trip is as expensive as a weekend trip. cheap

   ______________________________

   ______________________________

____/6

____/25

# Class test 1

→ after Unit 1

LISTENING

## 1 After the trip to Wales

1 ⊙ *Listen to the conversation between Tim and Carl. Are the statements true or false? Tick ✔ the correct answer.*

| | true | false |
|---|---|---|
| 1. Carl enjoyed the class trip. | ☐ | ☐ |
| 2. Tim loves swimming in cold water. | ☐ | ☐ |
| 3. All of the students went swimming in a lake. | ☐ | ☐ |
| 4. Tim and Carl were not in the same boat. | ☐ | ☐ |
| 5. There was a monster under Tim's boat. | ☐ | ☐ |
| 6. Tim felt silly because he believed Mr Harmer. | ☐ | ☐ |

______/6

WRITING

## 2 Tim's day

*Look at the grid and write six sentences about what Tim did and didn't do yesterday.*

| Did Tim … | ☺ | ☹ |
|---|---|---|
| … go to school? | | ✔ |
| … go on a school trip? | ✔ | |
| … play games on the coach? | ✔ | |
| … sing songs on the coach? | | ✔ |
| … talk to the coach driver? | ✔ | |
| … sit next to his best friend Carl? | | ✔ |
| … have a lot of fun on the coach? | ✔ | |
| … enjoy all of the day? | | ✔ |

*Yesterday Tim didn't go to school because* ______________________

______________________

______________________

______________________

______________________

______/12

READING

## 3 An e-mail to Holly

*Read the e-mail. Write down in which line(s) you find the information.*

**From:** Lisa Masood

**To:** Holly Richardson | **Address book**

**Subject:** Red Nose Day

Hi Holly,

Thanks for sending me pictures of your Red Nose Day. They look great! At my school we had an "Embarrassing Outfit Day". Everyone wore something embarrassing or funny with red noses, of course. Lots of people wore a clown outfit and some people went to school in their pyjamas.

Our teacher, Mrs Cook, wore a pink mouse outfit. Now that really was embarrassing! She looked like a little girl, but she is 52 years old! Mr Andrews, my sister's teacher, wore a teddy bear outfit and that was very silly too.

Our families and friends gave us lots of money at the end of the day. It's for a children's charity in Bangladesh.

And what about me? Well, I was a sheep. A sheep? Yes, I wore a big white hat and I said "Baa baa!" all day. It was all really funny.

See you soon.

Love,

Lisa

| | line(s) |
|---|---|
| 1. Lisa got some photos from Holly. | *2* |
| 2. Holly and Lisa don't go to the same school. | |
| 3. Students at Lisa's school didn't wear uniforms on Red Nose Day. | |
| 4. Mrs Cook is not very young. | |
| 5. Mr Andrews is not Lisa's teacher. | |
| 6. The students and teachers raised a lot of money. | |
| 7. The money is not for Lisa's school. | |
| 8. Lisa enjoyed Red Nose Day. | |

_____ /7

_____ /25

# Class test 2 → after Unit 1

LISTENING

## 1 A bed in a tree

2 ⦾ *Listen to Carl and complete the text.*

Carl was in a forest. It was ____________ and dark and the mountain was ____________ . Carl felt very ____________ . He made a bed in a tree, but there were people in the forest and there was a lot of ____________ . There was a very ____________ man and his gloves were pink. Carl fell out of the tree, but that wasn't a problem because he was ____________ . It was all just a ____________ !

_____ /7

READING

## 2 The best

*Read the report in a school magazine and answer the questions. Write 1 to 4 words or numbers.*

### The best in the school
*by Diana Stoppard*

Who is the best singer in our school? Who is the funniest comedian or the best dancer? At the Red Nose Day talent show on Friday evening we found out.

Tara sang a song from a popular film. She was great and everyone clapped, but then Tim sang his song "Never go". He wrote it himself and it's a really good song. He's a great singer too. In the end he won the prize for best singer.

And the funniest comedian? We all know the answer: It's Lisa! She told us funny and crazy stories. One amazing story was about her awful day at an outdoor centre … we laughed and laughed. Sorry, boys – I know many of you think boys are funnier than girls, but that's not true in this school!
Carl won the prize for best dancer and that's not surprising. He was the only dancer! In our school dancing is not as popular as singing and comedy. I don't know why. Carl is cool and dancing is so much fun. So come on friends – let's see more dancing at next year's talent show!

1. What did they have at Diana's school on Red Nose Day? ____________
2. Did Tara win the prize for the best singer? ____________
3. What is special about Tim's song? ____________
4. Who told the funniest stories? ____________
5. How many people tried to win the prize for the best dancer? ____________
6. What must be better at the talent show next year? ____________

_____ /6

MEDIATION **3** **Which outdoor centre is better?**

*Your Welsh friend Dylan wants to go to an outdoor centre in Germany, but he can't understand everything in these two flyers. Read the flyers and answer Dylan's questions in English. Say what you think to answer his last question.*

## Wildfluss Abenteuerzentrum

Ein Wochenende lang in wunderschönen Bergseen und Flüssen schwimmen und rudern. Unter dem freien Sternenhimmel schlafen, zusammen draußen kochen, am Lagerfeuer sitzen, singen, erzählen, lachen … sich verzaubern lassen!
Bringt einfach einen Schlafsack, Proviant und gute Laune mit!
**Wochenendangebot** für Jugendliche von 12 bis 18 Jahren: 200 € pro Wochenende (Freitag 18 Uhr bis Sonntag 16 Uhr)

## Jugendcamp Kick

Verbringt ein Wochenende, eine Woche oder mehr Zeit im Jugendcamp Kick.
**Aktivitäten:** Fußball, Tennis, Rudern, Schwimmen, Wandern, Schluchtenklettern
**Unterbringung:** Berghütte mit Betten – naturnah aber bequem
**Verpflegung:** Unsere tolle Köchin Maria sorgt dafür, dass ihr nach einem spannenden Tag satt werdet.
**Preise:** pro Woche 590 €; pro Wochenende (Samstag 10 Uhr bis Sonntag 17 Uhr) 240 €

Dylan: Can you go to the outdoor centres just for a weekend?

You: ______________________________

Dylan: And is a weekend trip always from Friday to Sunday?

You: ______________________________

______________________________

Dylan: Which centre is more expensive?

You: ______________________________

Dylan: And where can I do the most sports activities?

You: ______________________________

Dylan: I want to sleep in a real bed. Is that possible?

You: ______________________________

Dylan: Which outdoor centre do you think is the best, and why?

You: ______________________________

______________________________

_____/14

Dylan: Hm, Kick sounds best for me.

_____/27

# Unit 2 Let's discover TTS!

## Test 1 → after Station 1

VOCABULARY

### 1 A royal house

*Put in the missing words. There are three extra words.*

architect | beautiful | build | design | husband | painting | Queen | space | upset | view

"Hello! I'm an ________________ and this is my new ________________. Look – it's a house for the ________________! She and her ________________ chose me for the job because I'm the best! The house is really ________________ and it has an amazing ________________ of the sea. I want to ________________ it soon."

_____ /7

VOCABULARY

### 2 School subjects

*Write the name of the school subjects under the pictures.*

1

History

2

________________

3

________________

4

________________

5

________________

6

________________

_____ /5

VOCABULARY

## 3 Ghosts in the hospital

*Complete the missing words.*

Lisa: Why is your little brother so sad?

Carl: He needs to go to the children's h _ _ _ _ _ _ _.

Lisa: Oh no! An angry queen once lived in that building and now there are g _ _ _ _ _ in there!

Carl: Lisa, that's not true. My brother is very u _ _ _ _ because he needs to go to the hospital. Don't tell him scary stories too!

Lisa: But he's i _ _ _ _ _ _ _ _ _ in history.

Carl: Your stories aren't history – they're just silly stories!

_____ /4

LANGUAGE

## 4 Presentations about kings and queens

*Underline the correct **relative pronouns**. There can be more than one correct answer.*

My classmates and I made presentations **which / who** were about different kings and queens. I spoke about a king **that / who** lived 500 years ago. My friend George made a presentation about kings **who / whose** live around the world now. Mary was the person **that / whose** presentation I liked best. She talked about the homes **that / which** kings and queens live in today.

_____ /5

LANGUAGE

## 5 An e-mail to Jay

*Cross out four **relative pronouns** that you do not need in this e-mail.*

Dear Jay,
My new school is great. There are so many clubs and so many activities that you can do. People who like music and art love the school. And there's one club that everyone likes: the Dance Club. The teacher who organises it once danced in a Bollywood film! She's the teacher who I like best here – you know I love Bollywood! There are Science and Technology Clubs too for people who enjoy those things – not me! There's one other club that I think is interesting: the Camera Club. They go on trips and take great photos.
Well, how are you Jay? And how is Shahid?
George

Is the word after the relative pronoun a verb? Then the relative pronoun is a subject and you need it!

_____ /4

_____ /25

# Test 2

→ after Station 2

VOCABULARY

## 1 A garden project

*Match the sentence parts. Draw lines.*

1. The sun was …
2. The bees were …
3. We got …
4. Together we made …
5. George dug …
6. And Jenny fell off …

a) started.
b) a hole.
c) humming.
d) shining.
e) a ladder.
f) progress.

_____ /5

VOCABULARY

## 2 The City Farm Club

*Put in the missing words. There are two extra words.*

birds | corner | hammer | join | members | pond | welcome | wildlife

THE CITY FARM CLUB

Our club needs more ______________. So ____________ the City Farm Club now! We ______________ everyone who loves farm animals! Every Friday afternoon we work at the City Farm in Westwick Park. We meet at 2 p.m. Our next project is to build a new home for the chickens in a ____________ behind the ______________.

So come with us next Friday and bring your ________________!

_____ /6

LANGUAGE

## 3 The new boy

*Cross out the wrong words: **when** or **while**.*

Frank is a new boy in our class. He had his first day yesterday. I showed him the school **when / while** my friends were starting their lessons. **When / While** we went into the computer room, Mr Smith was talking to some students about the internet. We looked at the Art room **when / while** class 7B were drawing birds. Some students were working on a song **when / while** I showed Frank the recording studio. My classmates were learning French verbs **when / while** we went back to our class, and we sat down and joined them.

**While** comes before an action in progress so you use it with the past progressive.

_____ /5

LANGUAGE

## 4 What were they doing when the storm started?

*Yesterday these people were doing different things when a storm started. Write what they were doing. Use the **past progressive**.*

1

2

3

4

5

6

1. Carla was reading a book. ______________________
2. Mr Kelly ______________________
3. Mrs Kelly ______________________
4. Paul ______________________
5. Jenny and Lisa ______________________
6. Baby Joe ______________________

_____ /5

LANGUAGE

## 5 In the garden

*Complete the sentences with the verbs in the **simple past** or **past progressive**.*

“I was working in the garden with my family when some things ______________ (go) wrong. My brother hit his foot while he ______________ (dig) a hole. Mum was taking photos when she ______________ (fall) into the hole. And my dad broke his thumb while he ______________ (build) a dog's house.”

_____ /4

_____ /25

# Class test 1 → after Unit 2

LISTENING

## 1 Lisa and Diana talk about films

3 ⦾

*Lisa meets Diana in the cafeteria on a Friday.*
*Listen to the dialogue and tick ✔ the correct answer.*

| | Lisa | Diana | both |
|---|---|---|---|
| 1. She watched a film yesterday evening. | ☐ | ☐ | ☐ |
| 2. She wants to be a vet. | ☐ | ☐ | ☐ |
| 3. She loves James Bond films. | ☐ | ☐ | ☐ |
| 4. She doesn't know an actor called Polly McCane. | ☐ | ☐ | ☐ |
| 5. She thinks Daniel Craig is a good actor. | ☐ | ☐ | ☐ |
| 6. In the end she gets a bit angry. | ☐ | ☐ | ☐ |

_____ /6

READING

## 2 Mila's blog

*Mila's new school has got a website with blogs. Complete the sentences with 1 or 2 words.*

**Mila says** **5:28 p.m. 1st October**

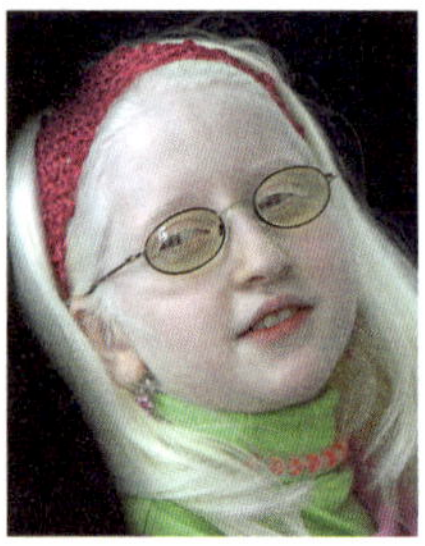

Hi everyone! My name's Mila and I'm new at Spring Hill School. I came from Germany to Wales this summer because my mum got a good job here and I love it! My favourite thing is swimming in the sea and there are fantastic places for swimming in Wales.
I started school here in September. I was a bit nervous about a new school, but Spring Hill is great. You can choose Film Studies as a school subject – wow! You can't do that in Germany. There are so many additional activities too. When I saw chess on the list, I thought, 'Who does that? Boring!' But then my new friend Ben told me he plays chess and it's really exciting, so why not? I want to be an actor, so the Drama Club is the club for me. We meet every Thursday and it's always lots of fun.
Another great thing about Spring Hill is that it's good for partially-sighted people here. Why is that important for me? Well, I can see people and big things, but I can't read a normal book. Teachers and students at Spring Hill help me a lot. I can usually just forget about my eye problems and enjoy life at my new school. I feel so welcome here – so this is a big THANK YOU!

1. Mila's mum got a new job in ____________________ .
2. Wales has a lot of amazing places to go ____________________ .
3. Before Mila started at Spring Hill School she felt ____________________ .
4. Mila has a new friend who plays ____________________ .
5. On Thursdays Mila goes to the ____________________ .
6. Mila has problems with her eyes: she is ____________________ .

_____ /6

MEDIATION

## 3 Which club?

*You are talking to your English friend Mark about what clubs you could join together. Read the information on the school website and answer Mark's questions in English.*

**Kepler-Schule**

**Aktuelles | Unsere Schule | Unterricht | Projekte und AGs | Kontakt**

**AG-Übersicht**

| Was? | Wann? |
|---|---|
| Sport<br>– Basketball<br>– Handball<br>– Fußball | <br>Fr. 15:00 Uhr<br>Mo. 15:00 Uhr<br>Di. 15:00 Uhr |
| Kochen<br>– französisch<br>– indisch | <br>Di. 15:00 Uhr<br>Di. 17:00 Uhr |
| Tanzen | Mi. 14:30 Uhr |
| Theater | Fr. 16:00 Uhr |
| Vogelbeobachtung | Fr. 15:00 Uhr |
| Zeichensprache | Do. 15:00 Uhr |

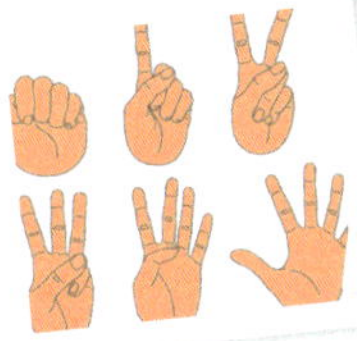

Mark: Are there any sports clubs?

You: ______________________________

Mark: Oh perfect: basketball, my favourite. When do they play?

You: ______________________________

Mark: And can you do music?

You: ______________________________

Mark: Hm, that's not really for me. I'm busy then. What about languages?

You: ______________________________

Mark: That's interesting, but I don't think I really need it. Are any of the other clubs surprising?

You: ______________________________

Mark: Really? Let's do birdwatching and basketball. Two clubs are enough, I think.

You: Well, there's a problem. ______________________________

_____/14

Mark: Oh no! Well, let's just join the Basketball Club then. OK?

_____/26

# Class test 2

→ after Unit 2

LISTENING

## 1 The Cooking Club

4 ⊙ *Listen to the conversation and cross out the wrong words.*

1. Rory's mum thinks Rory **is / isn't** interested in cooking.
2. He joined the Cooking Club because Lisa made a good **curry / presentation**.
3. At the club they cook **British / international** food.
4. Rory's mum **loves / doesn't like** Indian food.
5. The school's Cooking Club won a competition **yesterday / a year ago**.
6. They cook at **school / Lisa's house**.
7. Rory's mum thinks it's **good / bad** that he joined the club.

_____ /7

READING

## 2 The birdwatching trip

*Read the text. Answer the questions on page 27 in full sentences.*

*Dear Aunt Mia,*

*Thank you so much for my birthday present. I love the colour! I wore it on our last birdwatching trip on Saturday. We birdwatchers always need hats because we are outside so much, often in very bad weather!*

*The weather was awful on our last trip but that wasn't the main problem. We didn't see any interesting birds and a lot went wrong. It was funny.*

*First we went to the river where there are some cool birds and other animals. Diana saw something special – a big blue bird. She wanted to see it better, so she climbed a tree. That wasn't a good idea. She didn't see the bird and then she said, "Help! I can't get out of the tree!"*

*A man was working on his house near the river, so I asked him for his ladder. Then Mrs Walter, the instructor, climbed up the ladder to get Diana, but she fell off! Diana wanted to help her, but Mrs Walter was laughing and then she fell too! But don't worry, they're OK now.*

*The man with the ladder told us all about the blue bird and that was interesting, but while we were listening the bird came back and stole my lunch. What a silly day!*

*Thanks again and see you soon.*

*Love,*

*Tara*

1. What did Aunt Mia give Tara for her birthday? ______________________
2. What is Tara's hobby? ______________________
3. Was the weather good last Saturday? ______________________
4. Why did Diana climb a tree? ______________________

______________________
5. What was the man doing when Tara asked for help? ______________________
6. What did the blue bird do while the man was talking? ______________________

_____/12

WRITING

## 3 Carl's presentation

*Carl is making a presentation in class. You are taking notes because you want to give him some feedback. Look at the grid and write six sentences for Carl about his presentation.*

Start your sentences in different ways. Make sure you use linking words like "but", "and", "because", "also" and "so". Use phrases like "I think …", "I saw / noticed that …" and "I liked …".

| For a good presentation … | Did Carl do this? |
|---|---|
| … be on time. | ☺ |
| … introduce yourself. | ☺ |
| … smile and make eye contact with the audience. | ☹ |
| … speak with a clear voice. | ☺ but his voice was very quiet |
| … know your facts. | ☺ |
| … add a personal story. | ☹ |
| … don't read from your notes. | ☹ did this too much |
| … give the audience flyers. | ☺ good flyers |
| … say thank you to the audience for listening. | ☺ |

*Your presentation was interesting, but I think you were a bit nervous. You were*

______________________

______________________

______________________

______________________

______________________

_____/12

_____/31

# Unit 3 London is amazing!

## Test 1 → after Station 1

VOCABULARY

### 1 Around and about in London

*Write the names of these places.*

1. You can see lots of animals here. ______________________
2. This place is famous for street art and curry houses. ______________________
3. A museum where you can see buses and trains. ______________________
4. You can buy things and watch musicians here. ______________________

___ /4

VOCABULARY

### 2 Oyster cards

*Put in the missing the words. There are three extra words.*

credit | persuade | public transport | smartcard | top up | travel | wheelchair

If you want to ______________ around London for a few days, get an Oyster card. You can use an Oyster card on all ______________ in London and it is cheaper than normal tickets. Buy Oyster cards from Underground stations or from special shops and ________ them ________ when you need to. Two or three people can use the same ______________ if you are travelling together.

___ /4

VOCABULARY

### 3 How do I get to …?

*You are at Bond Street station and a tourist wants to go to Covent Garden. Look at the map of the Tube at the back of your book and tell the tourist how he can get there.*

Tourist: Excuse me. How do I get to Covent Garden, please?

You: ____________ the Jubilee line and go ____________ one stop. Get off at Green Park and ______________ the Piccadilly line. Go east and Covent Garden is the third ____________.

___ /4

LANGUAGE

## 4 What are they going to do this weekend?

*Look at the photos and write sentences about what the friends are going to do at the weekend.*

1

2

3

4

go shopping | read magazines | interview Jamila | go to a snack bar

1. Olivia and Holly are going to go shopping.
2. ______________________
3. ______________________
4. ______________________

____ /6

LANGUAGE

## 5 A weekend in London

*Jean lives in Wales. Complete the dialogue with her friend Mary with the correct form of the verbs. Use the* ***going-to future****.*

Mary: I 'm going to have (have) a birthday party next weekend. Do you want to come?

Jean: Yes, I'd like to come but I can't. I ______________ (visit) my cousins in London.

Mary: Wow, that's exciting! What ______________ (you / do) there?

Jean: Well, I want to see the Horse Guards and the Houses of Parliament. And we ______________ (go) to the British Museum and Buckingham Palace.

Mary: Oh, ______________ (you / take) lots of money with you?

Jean: No, I don't need a lot of money because all those things are free.

Mary: Really? But what about the Tube? That's expensive.

Jean: Well, we ______________ (not travel) by public transport.

We ______________ (go) by bike.

Mary: But it's December. What if the weather is bad?

Jean: Oh no. It ______________ (not be) cold.

____ /7

____ /25

# Test 2

→ after Station 2

VOCABULARY

## 1 The simple past: regular or irregular verbs?

*Fill in the missing form of the verbs and the German meaning of the infinitive form.*

| infinitive | simple past | German |
|---|---|---|
| 1. to beat | | |
| 2. | dealt with | |
| 3. | | *(be)folgen, hinterhergehen* |
| 4. to get off | | |
| 5. | meant | |
| 6. | | *fahren, reisen* |
| 7. to top up | | |

____/7

VOCABULARY

## 2 In Covent Garden

*What does **one** or **ones** mean in these dialogues? Write down the meaning.*

1. Holly: This shop has nice things. I love that hat there.
   Olivia: The red one?
   Holly: Yes, it's great, but it's expensive.

   one = *hat*

2. Jay: Let's watch the show outside. Some musicians are going to play soon.
   Amir: But I want to listen to the ones inside. They're really good. Can you hear them?
   Jay: Yes, I can and I think that music is boring.

   ones = ____________________

3. Jay: Come on! Let's go now. This is boring.
   Amir: But you're the one who wanted to watch these street musicians.

   one = ____________________

4. Olivia: Can you see the girl with the blue shoes?
   Amir: Oh, do you mean the tall one?
   Olivia: Yes, she's in our class.

   one = ____________________

____/3

LANGUAGE

## 3 A souvenir

*Amir wants to buy a souvenir. Complete the dialogue with **some** or **any** or one of their compounds.*

Seller: Can I help you?

Amir: Yes, I'm looking for ______________________ for my mother – a picture maybe.

Seller: I've got a nice painting of Covent Garden ______________________. Ah, here it is.

Amir: Yes, that's beautiful. How much is it?

Seller: It's £35.

Amir: Oh, have you got ______________________ cheaper?

Seller: I haven't got ____________ cheaper pictures, but I've got ____________ pens. They're £15 each.

Holly: I've got a better idea, Amir. _________________ can take a photo of you here in Covent Garden.

Amir: Yes, that's a much nicer present for my mum.

_____ /6

LANGUAGE

## 4 Interviews about Covent Garden

*Harry is interviewing Londoners and tourists about Covent Garden for the school magazine. He took these notes. Underline the correct words.*

Tourist:

I love it here. You can just sit and watch people, musicians and shows. You can also buy **something / everything** you want here: food, clothes, souvenirs ... It's great. It's my favourite place in the world! There's **nowhere / somewhere** like it.

Londoner 1:

Well, I come here when **anyone / someone** visits me who doesn't know London, but I don't really like it. There are people **everywhere / somewhere**. You can't walk **anywhere / somewhere** and **everything / something** is too expensive!

Londoner 2:

I think Covent Garden's fantastic. I feel like I'm on holiday when I'm here. OK, the shops are expensive, but you don't need to buy **anything / something**. You can just sit with a drink and a sandwich and watch some street theatre.

_____ /7

_____ /23

# Test 3 → after Station 3

VOCABULARY

## 1 At the Tower of London

*Look at the pictures and write down what they show.*

1. castle

2. ______________________

3. ______________________

4. ______________________

5. ______________________

6. ______________________

_____ /5

LANGUAGE

## 2 The London Eye

*Complete the text with the correct form of the words. Use* ***adjectives*** *or* ***adverbs****.*

### London Eye

If you want a ______________ (different) view of London, visit the London Eye. This big wheel is 135 m high and so you can see over a large part of London. The wheel moves very ______________ (slow) and you get on and off while it is moving. The whole trip is 30 minutes long – lots of time for some ______________ (good) photos. You can see ______________ (easy) through the big windows of the London Eye, but 25 people can travel with you and sometimes they stand between you and the view. If you want to enjoy the trip alone or just with your friends, you can pay extra, but it isn't ______________ (cheap)! The London Eye is open nearly every day. There are often queues so if you haven't got much time, buy your ticket on the internet.

_____ /5

# Green Line 2 G9

## Fit für Tests und Klassenarbeiten

Lösungsheft

Klett

# Unit 1 My friends and I

## Test 1

→ after Station 1

VOCABULARY

### 1 The noticeboard

*Read the flyer on the noticeboard. Put in the missing words. There are two extra words.*

ago | also | best | enjoy | month ✔ | raise | sale | think of

Next month it's that time again – time to raise money for children in our town. But what can we do? One year ago we had a great cake sale. Now we need a new activity. Can you think of a new idea? The best suggestion wins a prize! Write your ideas and your name here:

| Name | Year | Idea |
|---|---|---|
| | | |
| | | |

___/5

VOCABULARY

### 2 The school sale

*Look at the picture. Label the things and complete the text on the sign.*

___/5





LANGUAGE

### 3 Regular simple past forms

*Write the **simple past** form of the verbs.*

Watch the spelling of a verb before you add the **simple past** ending.

1. love loved
2. start started
3. clap clapped
4. plan planned
5. try tried
6. watch watched

___/5

LANGUAGE

### 4 The street show

*Complete the dialogue with the verbs in the **simple past**. There are regular and irregular verbs.*

Luke: We had (have) so much fun yesterday.

Dave: Why?

Luke: We did (do) a little comedy show on Church Street in Greenwich.

Dave: That sounds great!

Luke: It was! Olivia played (play) the saxophone, Jay and I danced (dance) and Holly collected (collect) money.

Dave: But that isn't comedy!

Luke: Oh, it was (be) funny. We all wore (wear) red noses and silly clothes. Sherlock jumped (jump) over boxes and chased (chase) his tail. People laughed (laugh) a lot!

___/9

___/24

## Test 2

→ after Station 2

VOCABULARY

### 1 A job puzzle

*Read the clues and write the words in the puzzle.*

Across →
3. He or she works with students in a school.
5. He brings parcels to your house.
6. This person sings in a music band.

Down ↓
1. He or she looks after animals like chickens and pigs.
2. You need him or her when your car has a problem.
4. This person takes people to other places in a taxi, bus or coach.

___/6

VOCABULARY

### 2 Dave's dream

*Put in the missing words. There are three extra words.*

arrest | friendly | missing | month | police | solution | someone | taxi

"In my dream a man called the police and said, "You must find Dave – he's dangerous!" They tried to arrest me! I jumped into a taxi and we went away fast. The driver was friendly. I forgot my problems and opened a window, but then someone saw me and said, "Hey, there's that dangerous boy!" I was really happy when the dream finished!"

___/5

LANGUAGE

### 3 Where was Jay?

*Complete the dialogue with the correct simple past form of **do** or **be**.*

1. Was Jay at school yesterday? – No, he wasn't.
2. Did he stay at home? – No, he didn't.
3. Did he have fun? – Yes, he did.
4. Was he with Holly? – Yes, he was.
5. Were they at the park? – Yes, they were!

First complete the questions and underline the verbs in the questions. Then write the short answers.

___/4





LANGUAGE

### 4 Where did you go?

*Complete the questions with the correct question word and form of the verb.*

how | what | when | where ✔ | who | why

1. Where did you go (you / go) on Sunday? – I went to the swimming pool.
2. Who did you go (you / go) with? – With Dave.
3. How did you get (you / get) there? – By bus.
4. Why did you go (you / go)? – Because we were bored.
5. What did you do (you / do) there? – We jumped into the water, of course!
6. When did you come (you / come) home? – At 6 p.m.

___/5

LANGUAGE

### 5 Olivia did, but Luke didn't

*Olivia had a busy day yesterday, but Luke did nothing. Write sentences about Luke.*

Before you write a sentence about Luke underline the verb in the sentence about Olivia.

1. Olivia tidied her room. — Luke didn't tidy his room.
2. Olivia went cycling. — Luke didn't go cycling.
3. Olivia made a cake. — Luke didn't make a cake.
4. Olivia did her homework. — Luke didn't do his homework.
5. Olivia saw her friends. — Luke didn't see his friends.
6. Olivia was tired in the evening. — Luke wasn't tired in the evening.

___/5

___/25

# Test 3 → after Station 3

VOCABULARY

## 1 Dave's e-mail

*Read the e-mail from Dave to his friend Tim. Put in the missing words. There are three extra words.*

adventure | Celtic | confident | course | forests | gorge scrambling
mountains | outdoor | tall | Wales | walking

Hi Tim,

Sorry, but I can't meet you on Friday. Our class wants to go to an outdoor centre in Wales. It's in a national park with forests and high mountains but … well, you know I'm not really into sports! We can do gorge scrambling there. What's that? I hope it's not too hard. I don't feel very confident about it. Walking in the mountains is OK but climbing? Well, it's all a big adventure!

See you next week,

Dave

___ /8

LANGUAGE

## 2 The highest mountain

*Look at the pictures and the words. Write the adjectives in the correct form.*

1.

high
higher
the highest

2.

fast
faster
the fastest

3.

easy
easier
the easiest

4.
80 people love this — popular
160 people love this — more popular
490 people love this — the most popular

___ /6





LANGUAGE

## 3 Comments on the class trip

*Put in the correct* comparative *or* superlative *forms.*

"This year's class trip was better (good) than the trip last year. For me gorge scrambling was the most exciting (exciting) activity. It was also the hardest (hard) challenge on the trip."

"Holly, Dave and I fell into the river. The water was colder (cold) than the sea! I felt cold for the whole day. For me that was the worst (bad) thing about the trip."

___ /5

LANGUAGE

## 4 That's not right!

*Correct the information. Write two sentences with different adjectives.*

1. Wales is as big as Germany. — small
   No, Wales is not as big as Germany.
   Wales is smaller than Germany.
2. Walking is as hard as climbing. — easy
   No, walking is not as hard as climbing.
   Walking is easier than climbing.
3. Dave is as confident as Jay. — nervous
   No, Dave is not as confident as Jay.
   Dave is more nervous than Jay.
4. A day trip is as expensive as a weekend trip. — cheap
   No, a day trip is not as expensive as a weekend trip.
   A day trip is cheaper than a weekend trip.

___ /6

___ /25

# Class test 1 → after Unit 1

LISTENING

## 1 After the trip to Wales

1 CD-ROM*

*Listen to the conversation between Tim and Carl. Are the statements true or false? Tick ✔ the correct answer.*

| | true | false |
|---|---|---|
| 1. Carl enjoyed the class trip. | ✔ | |
| 2. Tim loves swimming in cold water. | | ✔ |
| 3. All of the students went swimming in a lake. | | ✔ |
| 4. Tim and Carl were not in the same boat. | ✔ | |
| 5. There was a monster under Tim's boat. | | ✔ |
| 6. Tim felt silly because he believed Mr Harmer. | ✔ | |

___ /6

WRITING

## 2 Tim's day

*Look at the grid and write six sentences about what Tim did and didn't do yesterday.*

| Did Tim … | | |
|---|---|---|
| … go to school? | | ✔ |
| … go on a school trip? | ✔ | |
| … play games on the coach? | ✔ | |
| … sing songs on the coach? | | ✔ |
| … talk to the coach driver? | ✔ | |
| … sit next to his best friend Carl? | | ✔ |
| … have a lot of fun on the coach? | ✔ | |
| … enjoy all of the day? | | ✔ |

Yesterday Tim didn't go to school because Lösungsvorschlag: he went on a school trip. He played games on the coach with his friends. But he didn't sing songs. Then he talked to the coach driver. Tim didn't sit next to his best friend Carl. They had a lot of fun on the coach, but Tim didn't enjoy all of the day.

___ /12





READING

## 3 An e-mail to Holly

*Read the e-mail. Write down in which line(s) you find the information.*

**From:** Lisa Masood
**To:** Holly Richardson | **Address book**
**Subject:** Red Nose Day

Hi Holly,
Thanks for sending me pictures of your Red Nose Day. They look great! At my school we had an "Embarrassing Outfit Day". Everyone wore something embarrassing or funny with red noses, of course. Lots of people wore a clown outfit and some people went to school in their pyjamas.
Our teacher, Mrs Cook, wore a pink mouse outfit. Now that really was embarrassing! She looked like a little girl, but she is 52 years old! Mr Andrews, my sister's teacher, wore a teddy bear outfit and that was very silly too.
Our families and friends gave us lots of money at the end of the day. It's for a children's charity in Bangladesh.
And what about me? Well, I was a sheep. A sheep? Yes, I wore a big white hat and I said "Baa baa!" all day. It was all really funny.
See you soon.
Love,
Lisa

| | line(s) |
|---|---|
| 1. Lisa got some photos from Holly. | 2 |
| 2. Holly and Lisa don't go to the same school. | 3 |
| 3. Students at Lisa's school didn't wear uniforms on Red Nose Day. | 3–4 |
| 4. Mrs Cook is not very young. | 7–8 |
| 5. Mr Andrews is not Lisa's teacher. | 8 |
| 6. The students and teachers raised a lot of money. | 10 |
| 7. The money is not for Lisa's school. | 11 |
| 8. Lisa enjoyed Red Nose Day. | 13 |

___ /7

___ /25

* Dieses Symbol bedeutet, dass sich das Transkript zu der Aufgabe auf der CD-ROM befindet.

# Class test 2 → after Unit 1

LISTENING **1** A bed in a tree

2 *Listen to Carl and complete the text.*

CD-ROM

Carl was in a forest. It was cold and dark and the mountain was high. Carl felt very tired. He made a bed in a tree, but there were people in the forest and there was a lot of noise. There was a very tall man and his gloves were pink. Carl fell out of the tree, but that wasn't a problem because he was asleep/lucky. It was all just a dream!

____ /7

READING **2** The best

*Read the report in a school magazine and answer the questions. Write 1 to 4 words or numbers.*

**The best in the school**
*by Diana Stoppard*

Who is the best singer in our school? Who is the funniest comedian or the best dancer? At the Red Nose Day talent show on Friday evening we found out.

Tara sang a song from a popular film. She was great and everyone clapped, but then Tim sang his song "Never go". He wrote it himself and it's a really good song. He's a great singer too. In the end he won the prize for best singer.

And the funniest comedian? We all know the answer: It's Lisa! She told us funny and crazy stories. One amazing story was about her awful day at an outdoor centre … we laughed and laughed. Sorry, boys – I know many of you think boys are funnier than girls, but that's not true in this school! Carl won the prize for best dancer and that's not surprising. He was the only dancer! In our school dancing is not as popular as singing and comedy. I don't know why. Carl is cool and dancing is so much fun. So come on friends – let's see more dancing at next year's talent show!

1. What did they have at Diana's school on Red Nose Day? a talent show
2. Did Tara win the prize for the best singer? No, she didn't. / No, Tim won it.
3. What is special about Tim's song? He wrote it (himself).
4. Who told the funniest stories? Lisa
5. How many people tried to win the prize for the best dancer? 1
6. What must be better at the talent show next year? more dancing

____ /6





MEDIATION **3** Which outdoor centre is better?

*Your Welsh friend Dylan wants to go to an outdoor centre in Germany, but he can't understand everything in these two flyers. Read the flyers and answer Dylan's questions in English. Say what you think to answer his last question.*

**Wildfluss Abenteuerzentrum**

Ein Wochenende lang in wunderschönen Bergseen und Flüssen schwimmen und rudern. Unter dem freien Sternenhimmel schlafen, zusammen draußen kochen, am Lagerfeuer sitzen, singen, erzählen, lachen … sich verzaubern lassen!
Bringt einfach einen Schlafsack, Proviant und gute Laune mit!
**Wochenendangebot** für Jugendliche von 12 bis 18 Jahren: 200 € pro Wochenende (Freitag 18 Uhr bis Sonntag 16 Uhr)

**Jugendcamp Kick**

Verbringt ein Wochenende, eine Woche oder mehr Zeit im Jugendcamp Kick.
**Aktivitäten:** Fußball, Tennis, Rudern, Schwimmen, Wandern, Schluchtenklettern
**Unterbringung:** Berghütte mit Betten – naturnah aber bequem
**Verpflegung:** Unsere tolle Köchin Maria sorgt dafür, dass ihr nach einem spannenden Tag satt werdet.
**Preise:** pro Woche 590 €; pro Wochenende (Samstag 10 Uhr bis Sonntag 17 Uhr) 240 €

Dylan: Can you go to the outdoor centres just for a weekend?
You: Lösungsvorschlag: Yes, you can.
Dylan: And is a weekend trip always from Friday to Sunday?
You: At Wildfluss it's Friday evening to Sunday afternoon, but at Kick it's Saturday and Sunday.
Dylan: Which centre is more expensive?
You: Kick is more expensive. It's €240 for only two days.
Dylan: And where can I do the most sports activities?
You: Kick has the most sports activities. (Wildfluss only has swimming and boats.)
Dylan: I want to sleep in a real bed. Is that possible?
You: At Kick you sleep in a bed, but at Wildfluss you sleep outside.
Dylan: Which outdoor centre do you think is the best, and why?
You: I think Kick is better because you can do more sport(s) and you have good food and a bed. / Wildfluss is the best because it's cheaper and you can sleep outside. For me that's fun.
Dylan: Hm, Kick sounds best for me.

____ /14

____ /27

# Unit 2 Let's discover TTS!

## Test 1 → after Station 1

VOCABULARY **1** A royal house

*Put in the missing words. There are three extra words.*

architect | beautiful | build | design | husband | painting | Queen | space | upset | view

"Hello! I'm an architect and this is my new design. Look – it's a house for the Queen! She and her husband chose me for the job because I'm the best! The house is really beautiful and it has an amazing view of the sea. I want to build it soon."

____ /7

VOCABULARY **2** School subjects

*Write the name of the school subjects under the pictures.*

1 History

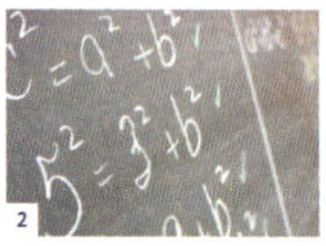

2 Maths

3 Science

4 French

5 PE / Physical Education

6 RE / Religious Education

____ /5





VOCABULARY **3** Ghosts in the hospital

*Complete the missing words.*

Lisa: Why is your little brother so sad?
Carl: He needs to go to the children's h o s p i t a l.
Lisa: Oh no! An angry queen once lived in that building and now there are g h o s t s in there!
Carl: Lisa, that's not true. My brother is very u p s e t because he needs to go to the hospital. Don't tell him scary stories too!
Lisa: But he's i n t e r e s t e d in history.
Carl: Your stories aren't history – they're just silly stories!

____ /4

LANGUAGE **4** Presentations about kings and queens

*Underline the correct **relative pronouns**. There can be more than one correct answer.*

My classmates and I made presentations **which / who** were about different kings and queens. I spoke about a king **that / who** lived 500 years ago. My friend George made a presentation about kings **who / whose** live around the world now. Mary was the person **that / whose** presentation I liked best. She talked about the homes **that / which** kings and queens live in today.

____ /5

LANGUAGE **5** An e-mail to Jay

*Cross out four **relative pronouns** that you do not need in this e-mail.*

Dear Jay,
My new school is great. There are so many clubs and so many activities ~~that~~ you can do. People who like music and art love the school. And there's one club ~~that~~ everyone likes: the Dance Club. The teacher who organises it once danced in a Bollywood film! She's the teacher ~~who~~ I like best here – you know I love Bollywood! There are Science and Technology Clubs too for people who enjoy those things – not me! There's one other club ~~that~~ I think is interesting: the Camera Club. They go on trips and take great photos.
Well, how are you Jay? And how is Shahid?
George

____ /4

____ /25

# Test 2

→ after Station 2

VOCABULARY

## 1 A garden project

*Match the sentence parts. Draw lines.*

1. The sun was …
2. The bees were …
3. We got …
4. Together we made …
5. George dug …
6. And Jenny fell off …

a) started.
b) a hole.
c) humming.
d) shining.
e) a ladder.
f) progress.

___/5

VOCABULARY

## 2 The City Farm Club

*Put in the missing words. There are two extra words.*

birds | corner | hammer | join | members | pond | welcome | wildlife

THE CITY FARM CLUB

Our club needs more members. So join the City Farm Club now! We welcome everyone who loves farm animals! Every Friday afternoon we work at the City Farm in Westwick Park. We meet at 2 p.m. Our next project is to build a new home for the chickens in a corner behind the pond. So come with us next Friday and bring your hammer!

___/6

LANGUAGE

## 3 The new boy

*Cross out the wrong words: **when** or **while**.*

Frank is a new boy in our class. He had his first day yesterday. I showed him the school ~~when~~ / while my friends were starting their lessons. When / ~~While~~ we went into the computer room, Mr Smith was talking to some students about the internet. We looked at the Art room ~~when~~ / while class 7B were drawing birds. Some students were working on a song when / ~~while~~ I showed Frank the recording studio. My classmates were learning French verbs when / ~~while~~ we went back to our class, and we sat down and joined them.

While comes before an action in progress so you use it with the past progressive.

___/5





LANGUAGE

## 4 What were they doing when the storm started?

*Yesterday these people were doing different things when a storm started. Write what they were doing. Use the **past progressive**.*

1. Carla was reading a book.
2. Mr Kelly was digging a hole.
3. Mrs Kelly was listening to music.
4. Paul was putting up a bird house.
5. Jenny and Lisa were playing football.
6. Baby Joe was sleeping.

___/5

LANGUAGE

## 5 In the garden

*Complete the sentences with the verbs in the **simple past** or **past progressive**.*

"I was working in the garden with my family when some things went (go) wrong. My brother hit his foot while he was digging (dig) a hole. Mum was taking photos when she fell (fall) into the hole. And my dad broke his thumb while he was building (build) a dog's house."

___/4

___/25

# Class test 1

→ after Unit 2

LISTENING

## 1 Lisa and Diana talk about films

3 CD-ROM

*Lisa meets Diana in the cafeteria on a Friday. Listen to the dialogue and tick ✔ the correct answer.*

| | Lisa | Diana | both |
|---|---|---|---|
| 1. She watched a film yesterday evening. | ☐ | ☑ | ☐ |
| 2. She wants to be a vet. | ☐ | ☑ | ☐ |
| 3. She loves James Bond films. | ☑ | ☐ | ☐ |
| 4. She doesn't know an actor called Polly McCane. | ☑ | ☐ | ☐ |
| 5. She thinks Daniel Craig is a good actor. | ☐ | ☐ | ☑ |
| 6. In the end she gets a bit angry. | ☐ | ☑ | ☐ |

___/6

READING

## 2 Mila's blog

*Mila's new school has got a website with blogs. Complete the sentences with 1 or 2 words.*

**Mila says** **5:28 p.m. 1st October**

Hi everyone! My name's Mila and I'm new at Spring Hill School. I came from Germany to Wales this summer because my mum got a good job here and I love it! My favourite thing is swimming in the sea and there are fantastic places for swimming in Wales.

I started school here in September. I was a bit nervous about a new school, but Spring Hill is great. You can choose Film Studies as a school subject – wow! You can't do that in Germany. There are so many additional activities too. When I saw chess on the list, I thought, 'Who does that? Boring!' But then my new friend Ben told me he plays chess and it's really exciting, so why not? I want to be an actor, so the Drama Club is the club for me. We meet every Thursday and it's always lots of fun. Another great thing about Spring Hill is that it's good for partially-sighted people here. Why is that important for me? Well, I can see people and big things, but I can't read a normal book. Teachers and students at Spring Hill help me a lot. I can usually just forget about my eye problems and enjoy life at my new school. I feel so welcome here – so this is a big THANK YOU!

1. Mila's mum got a new job in Wales.
2. Wales has a lot of amazing places to go swimming.
3. Before Mila started at Spring Hill School she felt nervous.
4. Mila has a new friend who plays chess.
5. On Thursdays Mila goes to the Drama Club.
6. Mila has problems with her eyes: she is partially-sighted.

___/6





MEDIATION

## 3 Which club?

*You are talking to your English friend Mark about what clubs you could join together. Read the information on the school website and answer Mark's questions in English.*

**Kepler-Schule**

Aktuelles | Unsere Schule | Unterricht | Projekte und AGs | Kontakt

AG-Übersicht

| Was? | Wann? |
|---|---|
| Sport<br>– Basketball<br>– Handball<br>– Fußball | <br>Fr. 15:00 Uhr<br>Mo. 15:00 Uhr<br>Di. 15:00 Uhr |
| Kochen<br>– französisch<br>– indisch | <br>Di. 15:00 Uhr<br>Di. 17:00 Uhr |
| Tanzen | Mi. 14:30 Uhr |
| Theater | Fr. 16:00 Uhr |
| Vogelbeobachtung | Fr. 15:00 Uhr |
| Zeichensprache | Do. 15:00 Uhr |

Mark: Are there any sports clubs?

You: Lösungsvorschlag: Yes, there are. You can do basketball, handball or football.

Mark: Oh perfect: basketball, my favourite. When do they play?

You: They play on Fridays at three o'clock (in the afternoon) / 3 p.m.

Mark: And can you do music?

You: No, but you can join / go to the Dance Club on Wednesday afternoons (at half past two).

Mark: Hm, that's not really for me. I'm busy then. What about languages?

You: Well, you can learn sign language.

Mark: That's interesting, but I don't think I really need it. Are any of the other clubs surprising?

You: I think birdwatching is surprising. / I think birdwatching and cooking are surprising.

Mark: Really? Let's do birdwatching and basketball. Two clubs are enough, I think.

You: Well, there's a problem. They're at the same time on Fridays.

Mark: Oh no! Well, let's just join the Basketball Club then. OK?

___/14

___/26

# Class test 2 → after Unit 2

LISTENING **1** **The Cooking Club**

4 *Listen to the conversation and cross out the wrong words.*

CD-ROM

1. Rory's mum thinks Rory ~~is~~ / **isn't** interested in cooking.
2. He joined the Cooking Club because Lisa made a good ~~curry~~ / **presentation**.
3. At the club they cook ~~British~~ / **international** food.
4. Rory's mum **loves** / ~~doesn't like~~ Indian food.
5. The school's Cooking Club won a competition ~~yesterday~~ / **a year ago**.
6. They cook at **school** / ~~Lisa's house~~.
7. Rory's mum thinks it's **good** / ~~bad~~ that he joined the club.

____/7

READING **2** **The birdwatching trip**

*Read the text. Answer the questions on page 27 in full sentences.*

*Dear Aunt Mia,*

*Thank you so much for my birthday present. I love the colour! I wore it on our last birdwatching trip on Saturday. We birdwatchers always need hats because we are outside so much, often in very bad weather!*

*The weather was awful on our last trip but that wasn't the main problem. We didn't see any interesting birds and a lot went wrong. It was funny.*

*First we went to the river where there are some cool birds and other animals. Diana saw something special – a big blue bird. She wanted to see it better, so she climbed a tree. That wasn't a good idea. She didn't see the bird and then she said, "Help! I can't get out of the tree!"*

*A man was working on his house near the river, so I asked him for his ladder. Then Mrs Walter, the instructor, climbed up the ladder to get Diana, but she fell off! Diana wanted to help her, but Mrs Walter was laughing and then she fell too! But don't worry, they're OK now.*

*The man with the ladder told us all about the blue bird and that was interesting, but while we were listening the bird came back and stole my lunch. What a silly day!*

*Thanks again and see you soon.*

*Love,*

*Tara*





1. What did Aunt Mia give Tara for her birthday? She gave her a hat.
2. What is Tara's hobby? She goes / likes birdwatching.
3. Was the weather good last Saturday? No, it wasn't.
4. Why did Diana climb a tree? She climbed a tree because she wanted to see / watch a special (blue) bird.
5. What was the man doing when Tara asked for help? He was working on his house.
6. What did the blue bird do while the man was talking? It stole Tara's lunch.

____/12

WRITING **3** **Carl's presentation**

*Carl is making a presentation in class. You are taking notes because you want to give him some feedback. Look at the grid and write six sentences for Carl about his presentation.*

Start your sentences in different ways. Make sure you use linking words like "but", "and", "because", "also" and "so". Use phrases like "I think …", "I saw / noticed that …" and "I liked …".

| For a good presentation … | Did Carl do this? |
|---|---|
| … be on time. | ☺ |
| … introduce yourself. | ☺ |
| … smile and make eye contact with the audience. | ☹ |
| … speak with a clear voice. | ☺ but his voice was very quiet |
| … know your facts. | ☺ |
| … add a personal story. | ☹ |
| … don't read from your notes. | ☹ did this too much |
| … give the audience flyers. | ☺ good flyers |
| … say thank you to the audience for listening. | ☺ |

*Your presentation was interesting, but I think you were a bit nervous. You were*

Lösungsvorschlag: on time and introduced yourself at the beginning. I noticed that you were nervous because you didn't smile and you didn't make eye contact with the audience. Your voice was also very quiet and you read from your notes too much. I saw that you knew your facts. You gave the audience (good) flyers with the facts, but you didn't add a personal story. At the end you said "Thank you for listening," so that was good.

____/12

____/31

# Unit 3 London is amazing!

## Test 1 → after Station 1

VOCABULARY **1** **Around and about in London**

*Write the names of these places.*

1. You can see lots of animals here. London Zoo
2. This place is famous for street art and curry houses. Brick Lane
3. A museum where you can see buses and trains. Transport Museum
4. You can buy things and watch musicians here. Covent Garden

____/4

VOCABULARY **2** **Oyster cards**

*Put in the missing words. There are three extra words.*

credit | persuade | public transport | smartcard | top up | travel | wheelchair

If you want to travel around London for a few days, get an Oyster card. You can use an Oyster card on all public transport in London and it is cheaper than normal tickets. Buy Oyster cards from Underground stations or from special shops and top them up when you need to. Two or three people can use the same smartcard if you are travelling together.

____/4

VOCABULARY **3** **How do I get to …?**

*You are at Bond Street station and a tourist wants to go to Covent Garden. Look at the map of the Tube at the back of your book and tell the tourist how he can get there.*

Tourist: Excuse me. How do I get to Covent Garden, please?

You: Take the Jubilee line and go south one stop. Get off at Green Park and change onto the Piccadilly line. Go east and Covent Garden is the third stop.

____/4





LANGUAGE **4** **What are they going to do this weekend?**

*Look at the photos and write sentences about what the friends are going to do at the weekend.*

1 go shopping

2 read magazines

3 interview Jamila

4 go to a snack bar

1. *Olivia and Holly are going to go shopping.*
2. Jay is going to read (some) magazines.
3. Dave and Jay are going to interview Jamila.
4. Luke and his mum are going to go to a snack bar.

____/6

LANGUAGE **5** **A weekend in London**

*Jean lives in Wales. Complete the dialogue with her friend Mary with the correct form of the verbs. Use the* ***going-to future****.*

Mary: I *'m going to have* (have) a birthday party next weekend. Do you want to come?

Jean: Yes, I'd like to come but I can't. I 'm going to visit (visit) my cousins in London.

Mary: Wow, that's exciting! What are you going to do (you / do) there?

Jean: Well, I want to see the Horse Guards and the Houses of Parliament. And we 're going to go (go) to the British Museum and Buckingham Palace.

Mary: Oh, are you going to take (you / take) lots of money with you?

Jean: No, I don't need a lot of money because all those things are free.

Mary: Really? But what about the Tube? That's expensive.

Jean: Well, we aren't going to travel (not travel) by public transport. We 're going to go (go) by bike.

Mary: But it's December. What if the weather is bad?

Jean: Oh no. It isn't going to be (not be) cold.

____/7

____/25

# Test 2
→ after Station 2

VOCABULARY **1** **The simple past: regular or irregular verbs?**

*Fill in the missing form of the verbs and the German meaning of the infinitive form.*

| infinitive | simple past | German |
|---|---|---|
| 1. to beat | beat | schlagen, besiegen |
| 2. to deal with | dealt with | sich befassen mit, umgehen mit |
| 3. to follow | followed | *(be)folgen, hinterhergehen* |
| 4. to get off | got off | aussteigen |
| 5. to mean | meant | bedeuten, meinen |
| 6. to travel | travelled | *fahren, reisen* |
| 7. to top up | topped up | aufladen |

____ /7

VOCABULARY **2** **In Covent Garden**

*What does **one** or **ones** mean in these dialogues? Write down the meaning.*

1. Holly: This shop has nice things. I love that hat there.
   Olivia: The red one?
   Holly: Yes, it's great, but it's expensive.

   one = hat

2. Jay: Let's watch the show outside. Some musicians are going to play soon.
   Amir: But I want to listen to the ones inside. They're really good. Can you hear them?
   Jay: Yes, I can and I think that music is boring.

   ones = musicians

3. Jay: Come on! Let's go now. This is boring.
   Amir: But you're the one who wanted to watch these street musicians.

   one = person / boy

4. Olivia: Can you see the girl with the blue shoes?
   Amir: Oh, do you mean the tall one?
   Olivia: Yes, she's in our class.

   one = girl

____ /3





LANGUAGE **3** **A souvenir**

*Amir wants to buy a souvenir. Complete the dialogue with **some** or **any** or one of their compounds.*

Seller: Can I help you?
Amir: Yes, I'm looking for something for my mother – a picture maybe.
Seller: I've got a nice painting of Covent Garden somewhere. Ah, here it is.
Amir: Yes, that's beautiful. How much is it?
Seller: It's £35.
Amir: Oh, have you got anything cheaper?
Seller: I haven't got any cheaper pictures, but I've got some pens. They're £15 each.
Holly: I've got a better idea, Amir. Somebody can take a photo of you here in Covent Garden.
Amir: Yes, that's a much nicer present for my mum.

____ /6

LANGUAGE **4** **Interviews about Covent Garden**

*Harry is interviewing Londoners and tourists about Covent Garden for the school magazine. He took these notes. Underline the correct words.*

*Tourist:*
*I love it here. You can just sit and watch people, musicians and shows. You can also buy **something / everything** you want here: food, clothes, souvenirs ... It's great. It's my favourite place in the world! There's **nowhere / somewhere** like it.*

*Londoner 1:*
*Well, I come here when **anyone / someone** visits me who doesn't know London, but I don't really like it. There are people **everywhere / somewhere**. You can't walk **anywhere / somewhere** and **everything / something** is too expensive!*

*Londoner 2:*
*I think Covent Garden's fantastic. I feel like I'm on holiday when I'm here. OK, the shops are expensive, but you don't need to buy **anything / something**. You can just sit with a drink and a sandwich and watch some street theatre.*

____ /7

____ /23

# Test 3
→ after Station 3

VOCABULARY **1** **At the Tower of London**

*Look at the pictures and write down what they show.*

1. castle

2. prison

3. raven

4. lion

5. bear

6. Beefeater

____ /5

LANGUAGE **2** **The London Eye**

*Complete the text with the correct form of the words. Use **adjectives** or **adverbs**.*

## London Eye

If you want a different (different) view of London, visit the London Eye. This big wheel is 135 m high and so you can see over a large part of London. The wheel moves very slowly (slow) and you get on and off while it is moving. The whole trip is 30 minutes long – lots of time for some good (good) photos. You can see easily (easy) through the big windows of the London Eye, but 25 people can travel with you and sometimes they stand between you and the view. If you want to enjoy the trip alone or just with your friends, you can pay extra, but it isn't cheap (cheap)! The London Eye is open nearly every day. There are often queues so if you haven't got much time, buy your ticket on the internet.

____ /5





LANGUAGE **3** **A true story!**

*Put in the missing words in the correct **adjective** or **adverb** form.*

careful | dirty | good | happy | hard | hungry | large | new | safe

Harrods once sold lions in their shop in London. In 1969 two Australians[1] who lived in London bought one and took it home to their flat. They called it Christian. Lions aren't dirty animals and they can live happily in a flat. Christian liked to play and the two men played with him. Even as a young lion he bit hard while he was playing, but the two men always played carefully and they still have all their fingers! Lions are usually dangerous, but the men believed that Christian was safe and they walked him in Hyde Park. But they were always careful and made sure that he was not hungry when they went out. When he was one year old Christian was already a large lion and the Australians decided that London was not a good place for him any more. So they took him to Africa and some animal experts helped him to live alone. Christian learnt well and a few years later, when the Australians visited him in his new home, he already had his own family.

____ /9

LANGUAGE **4** **How do they do it?**

*The friends do things differently. Complete the sentences with the correct **comparative forms**.*

Underline the adjective in the first sentence before you complete the second sentence.

1. Jay is a beautiful singer.
   He sings more beautifully than Luke.
2. Dave thinks most computer games are too easy.
   He beats the computer more easily than his friends.
3. Holly isn't a good swimmer. She can't swim as well as her friends.
4. Luke is a good football player. He plays football better than Dave.
5. Olivia likes loud music. She plays her music more loudly than her sister Lucy.
6. Olivia is a fast reader. She reads books faster than Holly.

____ /5

1 Australian [ɒsˈtreɪliən] Australier/in

____ /24

# Class test 1 → after Unit 3

VIEWING **1 London life**

*Luke and his cousin are in central London. Watch the film and tick ✔ the correct answer.*

CD-ROM

1. Luke and his cousin went …
   a) ☐ by bike.
   b) ☑ by boat.
   c) ☐ on a coach trip.
2. Big Ben has …
   a) ☑ 334 steps.
   b) ☐ 342 steps.
   c) ☐ 433 steps.
3. The people who built the London Eye came from …
   a) ☐ China and Pakistan.
   b) ☑ Germany and France.
   c) ☐ Poland and Canada.
4. They built Shakespeare's Globe in …
   a) ☐ 1799.
   b) ☐ 1979.
   c) ☑ 1997.
5. William Shakespeare came to London …
   a) ☐ 140 years ago.
   b) ☑ 400 years ago.
   c) ☐ 1,400 years ago.
6. The Tower of London is about …
   a) ☐ 150 years old.
   b) ☐ 415 years old.
   c) ☑ 950 years old.

____ /6

READING **2 Information from a website**

*Read the website. Take notes and answer the questions. If you can't find the answer in the text, write down the name of the link where you can find the information.*

Home | Where to find us | Special tours | Buy tickets online | What people say about us

THAMES BOAT TOURS

On our amazing tours you can see Big Ben, the London Eye, St Paul's, the Tower of London, Tower Bridge and many more of London's most famous tourist attractions. In good or bad weather you can enjoy your trip on our comfortable boats with toilets and a café which sells drinks and snacks.

**Boat tour times:** May – September: 9 a.m. to 5:30 p.m., every 30 minutes
October – March: 9 a.m. to 4 p.m., every 30 minutes
Open 7 days a week (closed 25th December). Tours take 45 – 50 minutes.

**Tickets:** Tickets cost £15 (£14) for an adult and £8.50 (£7.50) for a child.
Buy tickets on the boat or online (online prices in red).

1. How often do the boat tours go? every 30 minutes
2. Where do the tours start? link: 'Where to find us'
3. What time is the first tour of the day? 9 a.m. / 9 o'clock in the morning
4. What days can you go on a boat tour? Monday to Sunday / 7 days a week
5. Where can you buy the tickets? on the boat or online / on the internet
6. How much are the tickets for two adults and two children? £47 on the boat, £43 online / on the internet

____ /6





MEDIATION **3 The Shakespeare's Globe tour**

*You are in London on a tour of Shakespeare's Globe with your family. Your English is better than your parents'. Tell them what the tour guide said.*

"Hello and welcome to my tour of the world of William Shakespeare. First let me take you back to the year 1592 because it was in this year that Shakespeare first came to London. He was 25 years old when he left his wife and two children at home in Stratford-upon-Avon and went to live in London to make some money with his plays.
Remember what life was like in this time – there were no computer games, no TVs, no radios and no phones! So what did people do in the evening? They went to the theatre! Shakespeare's plays were already popular when he came to London and when he and his team built this theatre seven years later. They soon had audiences of three thousand. People who did not have much money also came here. They paid just one penny and stood here in the middle of the theatre. Others paid more and sat more comfortably.

Try to imagine what it was like. Not like our theatres today – the audience was loud and rude. They didn't sit politely and they laughed loudly too. And they threw things at the actors when they didn't like the play!
Shakespeare's plays were more popular than musicals today. They were funny and scary and exciting. Some people say that his plays were too good and they don't believe that he wrote them all. He was young when he came to London and he wrote a lot of plays and poems very quickly. How did he do it? Some people think that other people wrote Shakespeare's plays. They're not right if you ask me!"

*Also er sagt, dass Shakespeare 1592 nach London kam.* Lösungsvorschlag: Er war damals 25 Jahre alt, schon verheiratet und hatte zwei Kinder. Er ließ seine Familie in Stratford-upon-Avon zurück, um in London mit seinen Theaterstücken Geld zu verdienen. Da es damals noch keine Computerspiele, Fernseher, Handys usw. gab, gingen die Menschen ins Theater und Shakespeares Stücke waren schon beliebt / bekannt als er nach London kam. Das Theater wurde 1599 / sieben Jahre nachdem Shakespeare nach London ging gebaut. Schon bald schauten sich 3.000 Zuschauer die Stücke regelmäßig an. Der Eintritt kostete für einen Stehplatz nur einen Penny und für einen Sitzplatz etwas mehr. Im Theater ging es damals laut zu – die Zuschauer lachten und bewarfen die Schauspieler mit Sachen / Gegenständen, wenn ihnen ein Stück nicht gefiel. Manche Leute glauben, dass Shakespeare nicht alle Stücke selbst geschrieben hat, weil er so jung war und viele in kurzer Zeit verfasste. Der Führer meint aber, dass das nicht stimmt.

____ /18

____ /30

# Class test 2 → after Unit 3

LISTENING **1 Where do they want to go?**

5 a) *Listen to the four dialogues. Fill in the grid where the people want to go.*

CD-ROM

| They want to go to … | They get on the Tube at … | They get off the Tube at … |
|---|---|---|
| 1. Buckingham Palace | St. Paul's | Green Park |
| 2. the London Eye | Moorgate | Westminster |
| 3. the British Museum | Charing Cross | Holborn |
| 4. the Natural History Museum | Oxford Circus | South Kensington |

b) *Look at the map of the Tube at the back of your book and find the four Tube stations. Listen again and follow the routes on the map. Fill in at which station each person needs to get off the Tube.*

____ /8

READING **2 Welcome to the London Aquarium!**

*Read the text. Are the statements true or false? Tick ✔ the correct answer.*

The London Aquarium is one of London's most popular attractions and one of Europe's largest collections of fish and sea life. We are only a minute away from the London Eye so you can easily visit us on a day out to the city centre. But make sure you plan enough time! There are a lot of things to do here.
Find out about many different kinds of fish and sea life here. Which fish is the most dangerous? Which one swims fastest? What do they eat? You can also give food to the fish yourself. And are you brave enough to walk through a tunnel while sharks swim around you? One of the favourite attractions at the aquarium is our open pool full of rays. Put your fingers in the water and move them quickly and the fish come to you. What do the fish feel like? Come and find out!
If you want to have an extra special day, you can do a 'behind-the-scenes' tour and find out how we look after our animals. Or you can swim with the sharks! Of course, that costs extra and you must get your ticket a few days before.

| | true | false |
|---|---|---|
| 1. The London Aquarium has more fish than all other aquariums in Europe. | ☐ | ☑ |
| 2. You can walk there from the London Eye. | ☑ | ☐ |
| 3. You can give the fish some food. | ☑ | ☐ |
| 4. The sharks swim in a tunnel. | ☐ | ☑ |
| 5. You can feel some of the fish. | ☑ | ☐ |
| 6. If you pay more, you can swim with some fish in the aquarium. | ☑ | ☐ |

____ /6





WRITING **3 Things people left on the Tube**

*People often forget their things on the Tube. Look at the pictures, choose two of the things and write their story.*

Answer these questions:
- What happened?
- Who did the things belong to?
- How did the person leave them on the Tube?

Make sure that you use different sentence beginnings and linking words like "and", "because", "also" and "so".

Lösungsvorschlag: Picture 1: James travelled by Tube every day. He went to school by Tube and home again, and he also went to Football Club on Monday and Wednesday evening(s). One day he was going to Football Club and he was late, so he got ready for football on the train. Don't ask how he did it, but there weren't many people on the train that day. He put his clothes and his shoes in his bag or he thought he did. The shoes fell out of his bag and on the floor, but he didn't see them. Somebody found the shoes later.
Picture 3: Antony was an actor who had his first job in a theatre. He played a funny character who always stole money from shops, cafés or even friends. The first night of the show went very well and he was so excited that he took the money from the theatre home with him. Of course, it wasn't real money, but it looked real. A woman was sitting next to him on the train and saw the money. She thought it was real and she took it while Antony wasn't looking. At first the woman was very happy, but then she saw that the money wasn't real and got off the train quickly.

1

2

3

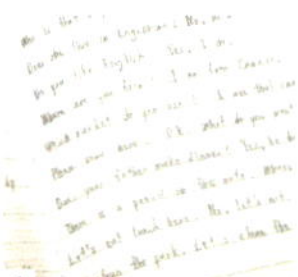
4

____ /28

____ /42

# Unit 4 Sport is good for you!

## Test 1 → after Station 1

VOCABULARY **1** **A puzzle**

*Look at the picture and write the names of the body parts.*

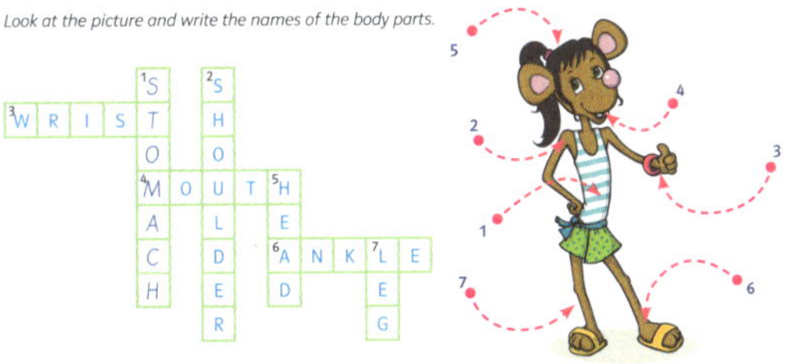


____/6

VOCABULARY **2** **Run for fun**

*Put in the missing words. There are two extra words.*

area | equipment | experience | health | in | right here | Run | running | until

**Run for fun!**

It's next Saturday right here at Spring Hill Sports Park: the Fun Run ! You love running so let us see how good you are.

We start at 10:00 a.m. It's not a marathon, but it's a long run through our beautiful area – just for fun. It's a great experience !

What equipment do you need? – Just good running shoes.

Who's in ? – You!

____/7





LANGUAGE **3** **A famous father**

*Complete the dialogue with the verbs in the **present perfect simple** or use short answers.*

be | break | lose | play | watch✔ | win

Rory: Have you ever watched a sports event in a stadium?

Tara: Yes, I have. My father plays rugby. He's really famous in the world of sports! So I 've been to a lot of rugby matches. Dad has never lost a game with me in the stadium.

Rory: Wow! And has your father won any important prizes?

Tara: Yes, his team won the Prince George Cup ten years ago.

Rory: And what about you? Have you ever played rugby? It's not really a girls' sport …

Tara: Hey! Women's rugby is great! But I know lots of girls who 've broken an arm or leg in rugby matches. It's not my thing. I love hockey.

____/6

Rory: But that's even *more* dangerous!

LANGUAGE **4** **What has happened?**

*Answer the questions with the correct words. Use the **present perfect simple**.*

she – win – a race | you – not do – your homework – yet | he – break – his arm | our team – not score – any goals – yet✔ | I – just – run – in a marathon

1. Why are you all so angry? – Our team hasn't scored any goals yet.
2. Why are you so tired? – I've just run in a marathon.
3. Why is Lisa proud? – She's won a race.
4. Why is Carl going to hospital? – He's broken his arm.
5. Why can't I play tennis now? – You haven't done your homework yet.

____/4

____/23





## Test 2 → after Station 2

VOCABULARY **1** **I don't feel well …**

*Look at the pictures and read what these people think. Complete the sentences.*

She's got a headache. He's got a backache. She has broken / hurt her leg. He feels sick.

____/4

VOCABULARY **2** **A bad day**

*Complete the missing words.*

I've had a bad day. I've t w i s t e d my ankle!

Oh no! Have you seen the d o c t o r ?

Yes. She gave me some o i n t m e n t to put on the ankle. It stops the pain.

I've had a bad day too. I've got a cough. I think I've caught a c o l d.

Do you have a f e v e r? Get a p r e s c r i p t i o n from the doctor and then go to bed.

I never take p i l l s.

But sometimes they really help.

____/7





LANGUAGE **3** **An accident**

*Underline the correct words: **just** or **yet**.*

"I've **just / yet** fallen off my bike. I can feel a pain in my leg, but I haven't looked at it **just / yet**. Maybe it's broken! I don't know. The accident has **just / yet** happened and I haven't been to the doctor **just / yet**."

____/4

LANGUAGE **4** **The runner's morning**

*Look at the pictures and the words. Write a question and an answer for each picture.*

1. have – breakfast
   Has he had breakfast yet?
   get up
   – No, he hasn't. He's just got up.

2. go – stadium
   Has he gone to the stadium yet?
   say – goodbye to his mum
   – No, he hasn't. He's just said goodbye to his mum.

3. race – finish
   Has the race finished yet?
   runners – start
   – No, it hasn't. The runners have just started.

4. win – race
   Has he won the race yet?
   race – not finish
   – No, he hasn't. The race hasn't finished yet.

____/9

____/24

# Test 3

→ after Station 3

VOCABULARY

## 1 Advice for Gwen

*Complete the e-mail to Gwen. There are three extra words.*

almost | award | cold | cramp | like | Player | runner | should | shouldn't

Dear Gwen,

I've heard you're running in the marathon trials. That's great!

I've never run in a marathon, but I play football. Last year my team had an important match. I wanted to win the award for 'Best Player'. I started really well, but then I got a cramp. It really hurt. I almost had to leave the match! Do you know what it's like? Well, it's awful and you should always warm up for a match or for a run, believe me.

See you soon!

Sam

___/6

LANGUAGE

## 2 Signal words

*Put the words in the grid.*

after that ✓ | before | ever | in 1998 | just | last week | two weeks ago | yesterday | yet

| You often use it with the simple past: | You often use it with the present perfect simple: |
|---|---|
| – after that | – before |
| – in 1998 | – ever |
| – last week | – just |
| – two weeks ago | – yet |
| – yesterday | |

___/8

The signal words for the **simple past** are usually for an action that started and finished in the past.
The signal words for the **present perfect simple** often show a link to the present.





LANGUAGE

## 3 An interview with Jay

*Underline the correct form of the verbs.*

Diana: Have / Did you ever run in a race, Jay?

Jay: Me? No, I 've never run / never ran in a race.

Diana: And have you ever won / did you ever win a sports award?

Jay: No, sports are not really my thing, but I won / have won a dance prize last year.

Diana: Ah! Which prize did you win / have you won?

Jay: It was / has been the 'Greenwich Young Dancer' award. I'm really proud of it!

___/6

LANGUAGE

## 4 A real marathon

*Ayla is now 18 and she ran her first full marathon yesterday. Put in the correct form of the verbs. Use the **simple past** or **present perfect simple**.*

never have ✓ | run ✓ | never be | feel | say | never see | be

2nd

I have never had as much fun as I had yesterday. I ran in a real marathon for the first time! Of course, it was very, very hard. I have never been so tired, but it was amazing. Yesterday evening I felt so good. My mother said, "I 've never seen a girl who looks as happy as you." She was right!

___/5

___/25

# Class test 1

→ after Unit 4

LISTENING

## 1 At the stadium

6 ◎ *Steven is a young football player who has just finished his first big match. Listen to the interview with a reporter and answer the questions. Write 1 to 3 words.*

CD-ROM

1. Has Steven had a lot of moments like this one before? No, he hasn't.
2. Does he think he is the best player on the team? No, he doesn't.
3. When the match started, was Steven scared? Yes, he was.
4. Where did Steven's father watch the match? in the stadium
5. Who has always believed in him? his parents
6. What is he going to do at nine o'clock this evening? go to bed / sleep

___/6

READING

## 2 The marathon website

a) *Read the website. Match the correct headings to the text. There are two extra headings.*

A How healthy must I be?
B What's the best way to start training?
C Who can run?
D When is the half marathon?
E Are there any other tips?
F Where can I get good running shoes?
G Should I stop training if my legs or ankles hurt?

Home | About | News | Where and when | Advice

C 1. Adults of 18 or older can run in the full marathon. Anybody of 12 years or older can run in the half marathon.

A 2. You must get fit before you run a long distance. A marathon is hard, and you should talk to your doctor about it first. A half marathon is hard too, but if you start with the training now, you can do it!

B 3. Start slowly. You should run often but not for too long. Four days a week for 30 minutes is a good way to start. Do you think that 30 minutes' running is too hard? Then walk – that's training too. Start running when you feel ready.

G 4. Yes, stop right away! Maybe it is not a big problem, but you should see your doctor and find out. Never run when your legs or ankles hurt. You can make a small problem into a big problem fast.

E 5. Wear good running shoes. In the marathon, use the shoes that you always wear for training. You should never wear new shoes on the day of the race.

___/4





b) *Look at the website on page 44 again. Are the statements true or false? Tick ✓ the correct answer. Which lines in the text tell you that the statements are true or false?*

| | true | false | line(s) |
|---|---|---|---|
| 1. Only adults can run in the full marathon. | ✓ | | 1 |
| 2. You should not run every day when you start training. | ✓ | | 6–7 |
| 3. You must run – walking does not help in training. | | ✓ | 8 |
| 4. Running can make a small injury worse. | ✓ | | 10–11 |
| 5. You should buy new running shoes the day before the marathon. | | ✓ | 13 |

___/4

WRITING

## 3 The match

*Holly has some questions about a match you have just played in. It can be a football, rugby or basketball match, or any other team sport. Write an e-mail to Holly and answer her questions.*

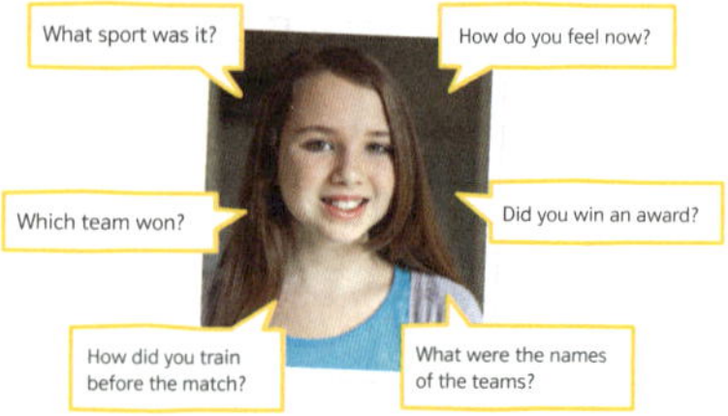


Dear Holly,

Lösungsvorschlag: I've just played in a fantastic basketball match.
My team, the BasketBirds, won. The other team, the Springers, played well, but we were much better and I was the best. So we won the game and I received the 'Best New Player' award! We trained every evening for three weeks before the match because we really wanted to play well. I wanted to win too, of course, so I'm very happy now!
Have you played basketball before? It's great!
What sport(s) do you like?
Love,
(your name)

___/20

___/34

# Class test 2

→ after Unit 4

LISTENING

## 1 At the doctor's

7 a) *Listen and put the pictures in the order they really happened. There is one extra picture.*

CD-ROM

___ /4

b) *Listen again and fill in the grid.*

| | Tara | Rory | Mr West |
|---|---|---|---|
| 1. Who had a sports accident? | ✓ | | |
| 2. Who hurt his or her hand? | | ✓ | |
| 3. Who has used ointment? | | ✓ | |
| 4. Who has got a pain? | ✓ | ✓ | ✓ |

___ /6

READING

## 2 The best

*Read the article. Copy 1–10 words from the text to show that the the statements on page 47 are correct.*

**We're the best!**

Now everybody knows: Our school is the very best! Well, we're the best at football! Last Sunday eight schools played in four exciting matches. Redhill School played against Lewis School, and did we win? Yes, we did: seven to one – what a score! And who won the award for 'Best Player'? – Tim, of course. Four of the seven goals were his. Tim, we're proud of you!

But the day wasn't perfect. Jimmy Waters twisted his ankle while he was trying to stop a goal. That evening, while the other team members were having a party and telling stories about the great match, Jimmy was at home in bed. Sorry, Jimmy! You were doing a great job when you twisted your ankle, and a party is always better when you are there. Next time!

The other thing that went wrong was very funny. One of the Newpark School players has got a 5-year-old sister whose name is Maria. She loves watching football and playing it. In the middle of the match she ran onto the pitch, caught the ball and kicked it into the goal! Fantastic, Maria – your goal was the best thing that happened on a great day!





1. Each school team played one match. eight schools played in four exciting matches
2. Tim's award is not a surprise. Tim, of course. Four of the seven goals were his.
3. Jimmy hurt his foot. Jimmy Waters twisted his ankle
4. Jimmy didn't go to the party. Jimmy was at home in bed.
5. Maria is a football fan. She loves watching football and playing it.
6. The fans loved Maria's goal. your goal was the best thing that happened

___ /5

MEDIATION

## 3 At the surgery

*Your Welsh friend Jenny is staying with you for a week. Today Jenny is sick and you take her to the doctor's. Tell Jenny what the doctor says in English and tell the doctor what Jenny says in German.*

You: Meine Freundin fühlt sich krank.

Doctor: Frage sie bitte, ob sie etwas Schlechtes gegessen hat.

You: Have you eaten anything bad?

Jenny: Well, I've eaten the same as you, but you aren't sick.

You: Nein, wir haben beide das Gleiche gegessen.

Doctor: Hat sie Fieber?

You: Have you got a fever?

Jenny: No, I haven't. I feel cold.

You: Nein, ihr ist (eher) kalt.

Doctor: Bitte sie, den Mund aufzumachen.

You: Open your mouth, please.

Doctor: Oh, alles rot. Offensichtlich hat sie eine schlimme Erkältung.

You: You've caught a (bad) cold.

Doctor: Sie sollte viel trinken und am besten im Bett bleiben bis sie sich wieder besser fühlt.

You: You should drink a lot and stay in bed until you feel better again.

Jenny: OK. Thanks for your help.

___ /12

___ /27

# Unit 5 Stay in touch

## Test 1

→ after Station 1

VOCABULARY

### 1 Texts, e-mails, profiles …

*Match the sentence parts. Draw lines.*

1. I text …
2. I receive …
3. On social networks I change …
4. I always post …
5. My brother plays …
6. And my mum checks …

a) about 20 texts every day.
b) her e-mails about ten times every day!
c) photos of my friends after a party.
d) my best friend every morning.
e) my profile very often.
f) video games all day.

___ /5

VOCABULARY

### 2 Tell Kate

*Put in the missing words. There are two extra words.*

agony – as soon as – care – face-to-face – forever – friendship – site – social – teen – worry

"I'm Kate – I'm an agony aunt and I work for a teen magazine. People write to me and tell me their problems. For young people, friendship is very important and most questions are about problems with friends. I don't think that social networks make teenagers' lives easier. They see photos online of friends who are having fun and they worry that they aren't part of the group. But you shouldn't believe everything you see online. The problems often go away as soon as people talk to each other face-to-face. Most people care about their friends and they want to help. So talk to your friends!"

___ /8





VOCABULARY

### 3 What's your advice?

*Tara is talking to her friends about their problems. Use the words and show understanding or give advice.*

1. Lisa: I'm so sad. My best friend is going to live in Canada.
   Tara: I'm sorry you're feeling upset. (sorry – feel – upset)
2. Rory: One of my classmates often posts awful pictures of me.
   Tara: My advice is to talk to him. (my advice – talk to him)
3. Anne: I feel so alone with my problems.
   Tara: Why don't you ask (your) friends for help? (why – not ask – friends for help)

___ /3

LANGUAGE

### 4 Kate's advice

*Underline the correct words.*

**This is my advice for teens who use social networks:**

⇨ Don't start to worry **whenever** / **before** you see a photo of friends who are laughing without you. It's just a picture of one moment.

⇨ **Because** / **Before** you make a person an online friend, make sure you know who he or she is.

⇨ Block a person **as soon as** / **until** you have a bad feeling about them.

⇨ Be extra careful when you post photos of yourself and others **because** / **after** you don't always know who sees them.

⇨ Don't act **until** / **like** you are too crazy or silly online. Not everybody knows you in real life!

___ /5

LANGUAGE

### 5 Carl doesn't have a girlfriend, does he?

*Complete the dialogue with the correct **question tags**.*

Anne: Hello. You're Carl, aren't you?

Carl: Yes, I am. But I don't know you, do I?

Anne: I'm Anne Rees.

Carl: Oh, Anne! My sister is your partner at the Tennis Club, isn't she?

Anne: Yes, she is. She has told me a lot about you. You've just won the prize for the 'Best School Blog', haven't you? Fantastic! And you don't have a girlfriend, do you?

Carl: Uh … no, I don't. Why?

___ /4

___ /25

# Test 2 → after Station 2

VOCABULARY

## 1 The broken bike

*Complete the missing words.*

**Olivia says** **12:15 p.m. 3rd April**

I'm going c r a z y! My bike is broken again and I can't f i x it. I've done it a m i l l i o n times before, but this time I don't understand it.

**Dave** 12:20 p.m. What on e a r t h is the problem?

**Olivia** 12:22 p.m. The wheels don't move.

**Holly** 12:24 p.m. Look for s t e p - b y - s t e p advice online. Or m a i l George (he can always help).

**Dave** 12:30 p.m. Who's George? I'm a g e n i u s and I can come to your house right away!

____/7

LANGUAGE

## 2 I'm not allowed to …

*Look at the photos. Complete the text with the correct form of* ***not be able to*** *or* ***not be allowed to****.*

"My dad is not able to use his new smartphone very well. I could help him, but he doesn't want my help."

"Once my phone was broken and I wasn't able to chat with my friends. I felt awful!"

"I 'm not allowed to use our computer at home after 8 p.m."

"My sister has got a tablet, but I 'm not allowed to go anywhere near it."

____/4





LANGUAGE

## 3 Technology and my family

*Complete the sentences with the correct form of* ***be able to, be allowed to*** *or* ***have to****.*
*Use the simple present or simple past.*

Look at the sentences and decide if you need to use "be allowed to" (= *dürfen*), "be able to" (= *können*) or "have to" (= *müssen*). Be careful: Sometimes you have to use the negative form!

1. I 'm allowed to have my first smartphone this year. My parents have said yes at last!
   I wasn't allowed to have one last year because Mum said I was too young.
2. My sister was able to use a computer when she was six. It was easy!
   She 's able to play video games on the computer very well now.
3. My brother and I don't have to ask our parents when we want to use the computer. We just use it.
   We had to ask when we were younger because we didn't know how to turn it on.

____/6

LANGUAGE

## 4 A new phone

*Cross out the wrong words.*

Ben: My new phone was very expensive. What if I lose it?
Paul: You ~~could / should /~~ **shouldn't** worry so much!
Ben: You're right. Hey, I'm bored. Let's go swimming.
Paul: Oh, sorry. I ~~'m allowed to /~~ **have to** ~~/ 'm able to~~ go home soon. I don't have much time.
You **could** ~~/ shouldn't / are able to~~ ask Rory.
He has time today.
Ben: Rory? Oh, … no. I can go alone.
Paul: Alone? Really? Well, don't take your new phone with you.
Ben: Why ~~aren't able to /~~ **shouldn't** ~~/ don't have to~~ I take my phone with me?
Paul: You **could** ~~/ should / have to~~ lose it!

____/5

____/22

# Class test 1 → after Unit 5

VIEWING

## 1 In the news

*Watch the film. Put the sentences in the correct order. Write the numbers (1–6) in the boxes.*

CD-ROM

- 4 A A young woman was on the bus when she heard about the new game.
- 1 B A reporter explains why people are standing in a queue.
- 6 C The reporter may try the game.
- 5 D A young man found out about the game when he was reading the newspaper.
- 3 E Holly texted Olivia about the new 'Fantasia' game.
- 2 F The reporter starts talking to Olivia.

____/6

READING

## 2 Thanks Kate

*Read Lenny's letter to the magazine* TeenSpeak. *Copy 1–10 words from the text to show that the statements on page 53 are correct.*

Dear *TeenSpeak*,

I want to say thank you to agony aunt Kate because she really helped me.

I was spending too much time alone with my smartphone and when I saw photos of my classmates who were having fun without me, I felt sad. People at school like me and say I'm clever, but they don't invite me to do things with them.

One day I saw a photo online of my classmates Jeff, Pam and Manisha. They were enjoying themselves at the boating lake. I love boats, but they are no fun alone. The photo was too much, so I wrote to Kate.

"Talk to them face-to-face," replied Kate. "Just tell them that you would like to go too. And remember: Everybody looks happy in the photos they post online but that doesn't mean they are having fun all the time."

I sit next to Jeff in History lessons so it wasn't difficult to talk to him. The next time I saw some happy boating lake photos I said, "Hey, did you have fun at the lake yesterday? You know, I love boats."
"Really? Why didn't you tell us before? Come with us next time!" said Jeff. "We were a bit bored yesterday. It's always just the three of us …"
"You were bored?" I asked. "But you looked so happy in the photos."
"Yeah," answered Jeff, "but everybody looks happy in the photos they post. We *have to* look happy, don't we? Sometimes it's hard work!"

Kate was right! Now I don't know why I felt so bad. Thanks Kate!

Lenny P.





1. Lenny felt bad when his friends had fun without him. *I felt sad*
2. Lenny wrote to Kate because of a photo. The photo was too much, so I wrote to Kate.
3. Kate said that Lenny should talk to Jeff, Pam and Manisha. "Talk to them face-to-face," replied Kate.
4. Jeff invited Lenny to go to the boating lake with him and his friends. "Come with us next time!"
5. Jeff is not always as happy as he looks in photos. "Sometimes it's hard work!"
6. Lenny feels better now. Now I don't know why I felt so bad.

____/5

WRITING

## 3 The new rule

*Read the information on the school noticeboard. Write an e-mail to Dave and tell him what the rule is, some things you can't do at school now and two reasons why you think the rule is good or bad.*

Think about phones at school. Make a list of reasons for and against them. Use those ideas for your e-mail.

**!!!!!! Important – Mobiles and smartphones at school !!!!!!**

Because students are using their phones too much in class and in the breaks, and because we have a problem with cyber bullies, we have made this new rule:

**You may bring your phone to school**

**BUT**

**you must turn it off for the whole school day!**

Dear Dave,

Our school has made a new rule about mobiles and smartphones.

Lösungsvorschlag: We can bring our phones to school, but we have to turn them off for the whole school day! We are not allowed to use them in class or in the breaks.

I think this new rule is awful because we can't use social networks or take photos at school any more.

Maybe some things are good. In the breaks we have to talk to each other face-to-face and sometimes that's more fun. We also had a problem with cyber bullies, but now the problem is better.

Anyway, I think this rule is too hard. What do you think?

Please write back soon.

(your name)

____/18

____/29

# Class test 2 → after Unit 5

LISTENING **1** **When Dad was young …**

8 ⊙ *Listen to the conversation and complete the sentences. Use 1 to 3 words.*

CD-ROM

1. Tim's dad is 50, but he doesn't feel old (at all).
2. Tim thinks that when his dad was a teenager, the world was very different.
3. In the past Tim's father made plans with his friends when he saw them face-to-face.
4. His dad didn't have a mobile, but he was able to call his friends at home.
5. Tim always calls his father when he's coming home late(r).
6. Tim is going to be his dad's first online friend.

___/6

READING **2** **A problem**

*Read the two e-mails. Look at the statements on page 55 and write down the numbers of the lines which give you this information.*

**From:** Diana Stoppard
**To:** Amy McNeil | **Address book**
**Subject:** Louise

Dear Amy,
Thanks for posting that nice photo of us and for your message. Posts and e-mails are OK, but life was better when you lived here in Bradford!
I've got a problem now and I'm writing you an e-mail because I don't want other people to read this. Yesterday was Louise's birthday and … I forgot it! She was really angry. "Amy never forgot my birthday," she said. "When Amy was here, we three were good friends, but now I know: You only liked Amy. I can find better friends than you. Goodbye, Diana!"
I'm so upset. I've lost you and now I've lost Louise. What should I do?
Di xxx

**From:** Amy McNeil
**To:** Diana Stoppard | **Address book**
**Subject:** Re: Louise

Dear Di,
Oh no! First, you haven't lost me! We're still friends. But you have to talk to Louise. I think she was just angry for one moment. You could send her a nice card and write "Sorry, I forgot your birthday!" on it. Then invite her to do something fun with you. Buy cinema tickets, for example. But Di – you've forgotten my birthday before too, more than once! Here's my most important advice: Put your friends' birthdays in your phone!
See you in the summer holidays.
Love, Amy





| | | line(s) |
|---|---|---|
| 1. | Amy doesn't live in Bradford any more. | 3 |
| 2. | Diana didn't write her problem as a comment on Amy's post. | 4 |
| 3. | Louise doesn't want to be friends with Diana now. | 7 |
| 4. | Amy thinks Diana and Louise should do something nice together. | 13–14 |
| 5. | Diana often forgets her friends' birthdays. | 15 |

___/4

MEDIATION **3** **The school's social network**

*Your Welsh friend Jack asks you about social network rules at your school. Read the information on the school website and answer his questions in English.*

Aktuelles | Unsere Schule | Klassen | Aktivitäten | **Schulregeln** | Kontakt

Unsere Schule hat ein lebhaftes soziales Netzwerk im Internet. Dieses benutzen wir, um über Neuigkeiten zu informieren und über wichtige Schulereignisse zu berichten. Schüler und Lehrer haben zudem die Möglichkeit, über die Seite miteinander zu kommunizieren, soweit beide Parteien das möchten. Lehrer dürfen aber nicht davon ausgehen, dass alle Schüler das Netzwerk jederzeit benutzen können oder wollen. Deshalb ist es z. B. nicht erlaubt, Hausaufgaben über das Netzwerk zu geben. Außerdem dürfen hier keine Noten diskutiert und keine persönlichen oder beleidigenden Kommentare geschrieben werden. Die Lehrer erklären sich bereit, Fotos von sich auf der Seite zu erlauben. Fotos von Schülern dürfen nur mit ihrer ausdrücklichen Erlaubnis hochgeladen werden.
Persönliche soziale Netzwerke darf jeder nach Belieben benutzen. Wir raten jedoch davon ab, dass Lehrer und Schüler Online-Freunde werden. Nach Ende der Schulzeit bietet dies eine Möglichkeit in Kontakt zu bleiben – davor empfehlen wir, Online-Kontakte nur über die Schulseite zu pflegen.

Jack: What kind of things does your school post on its social network page?

You: The school posts news and information about school events.

Jack: Does everyone have to use it? And do the teachers use it to give you homework?

You: No, we don't. Teachers aren't allowed to give us homework on the school's social network

Jack: Can you post photos of teachers and students?

You: Yes, you can post photos of teachers. But if you want to post photos of students, you have to / must ask them first.

Jack: What about your own social networks? Can you be online friends with your teachers?

You: You can use your own social networks, but you shouldn't be online friends with your teachers. You should use the school's social network for contact with teachers.

___/14

___/24

## Speaking → after Unit 1 (1)

PREPARE

### 1 Questions, questions

*Your friend was on holiday last month. Look at the words and write at least six questions about his or her holiday. Use the* ***simple past****.*

Where did you go? Did you Lösungsvorschlag: enjoy the holiday? Did you like (place / country)?
What did you do there? Did you have an adventure? How did you get there? What did you eat?
What did you see? Where did you sleep? When did you go? Who did you go with?

DIALOGUE

### 2 Where did you go on holiday?

*Make some notes about your last holiday. (The information can be true or not true.) Then ask and answer questions with a friend. Use the questions from exercise 1 and other questions.*

**Start:**
A: Hello Karen.
B: Hi Paul. Where did you go on your last holiday?
A: I went to the sea. And you, Karen? Where did you go?
B: I went to London!
A: Wow! What did you …?

If possible, do exercise 2 with a friend from school. Then do exercise 3 with somebody in your family who speaks a little English (your mum / dad / older sister or brother / …).

MONOLOGUE

### 3 Is it true?

*Tell your partner about your friend's holiday. In the end your partner says "Yes, that's true." or "I don't think that's true."*

Karen went to London on her last holiday. She got there by train … .

56 fifty-six

## Speaking → after Unit 1 (1)

DIALOGUE

### 2 Where did you go on holiday?

*Lösungsvorschlag:*

A: Hello Karen.
B: Hi Paul. Where did you go on your last holiday?
A: I went to the sea. And you, Karen? Where did you go?
B: I went to London!
A: Wow! What did you do there?
B: Well, I saw all the famous places like Big Ben, the Tower of London and Buckingham Palace.
A: And where did you sleep?
B: My aunt lives in London, in Oxford Street, so we stayed at her house. And you? What did you do on holiday?
A: Swimming, swimming and more swimming. It was great!
B: Did you have an adventure?
A: An adventure? No, I didn't, but I had a lot of fun. Did *you* have an adventure?
B: Yes! I saw a ghost in the Tower of London. A man said, "Please help me!" but then he walked through the wall and wasn't there any more.
A: Scary! What did you enjoy most in London?
B: I loved Brick Lane. I really like Indian food / curries so that was great. What did you eat on holiday?
A: We ate fish every day. My parents love fish, but it was too much. How did you get to London?
B: We took the train to Paris and then another train through a long tunnel / the Channel Tunnel. Did you go to the sea by car?
A: Yes, and it's a long way too. I was very bored in the car, but the holiday was good.

MONOLOGUE

### 3 Is it true?

*Lösungsvorschlag:*

A: Karen went to London on her last holiday. She got there by train, through the tunnel / Channel Tunnel. Her aunt has got a house in Oxford Street and she stayed there. She saw Big Ben, the Tower of London and Buckingham Palace, and she ate Indian food / curries in Brick Lane. She had an adventure at the Tower of London: She saw a ghost there!
B: Hm, … her aunt has got a house in Oxford Street and she saw a ghost? I don't think that's true.

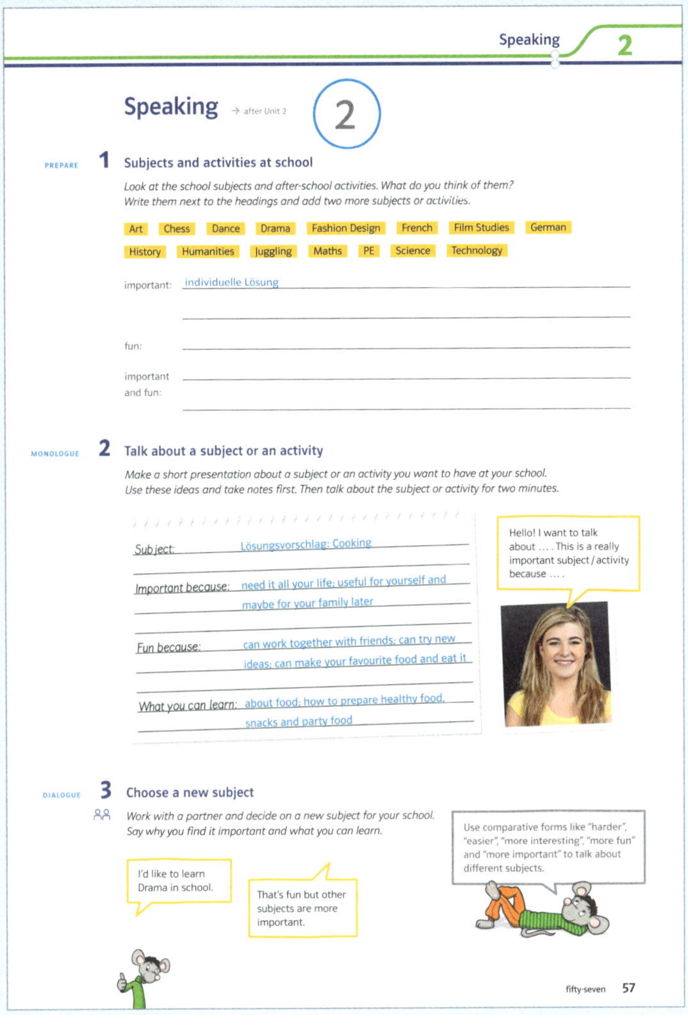
Speaking 2

Speaking → after Unit 2 (2)

PREPARE 1 Subjects and activities at school

*Look at the school subjects and after-school activities. What do you think of them? Write them next to the headings and add two more subjects or activities.*

Art | Chess | Dance | Drama | Fashion Design | French | Film Studies | German | History | Humanities | Juggling | Maths | PE | Science | Technology

important: individuelle Lösung

fun:

important and fun:

MONOLOGUE 2 Talk about a subject or an activity

*Make a short presentation about a subject or an activity you want to have at your school. Use these ideas and take notes first. Then talk about the subject or activity for two minutes.*

*Subject:* Lösungsvorschlag: Cooking

*Important because:* need it all your life; useful for yourself and maybe for your family later

*Fun because:* can work together with friends; can try new ideas; can make your favourite food and eat it

*What you can learn:* about food; how to prepare healthy food, snacks and party food



DIALOGUE 3 Choose a new subject

*Work with a partner and decide on a new subject for your school. Say why you find it important and what you can learn.*



fifty-seven 57

# Speaking → after Unit 2 (2)

MONOLOGUE

## 2 Talk about a subject or an activity

*Lösungsvorschlag:*

Hello!

I want to talk about Cooking. This is a really important subject because you always need it in your life. You need it for yourself and maybe later for your family. I also think it's a fun subject. You can do it together with friends and you can try new ideas together.

What's your favourite food? We can make it in the Cooking class! You also learn important things about food and you can learn how to make healthy things. And we can prepare snacks and party food … so many great things! Let's have Cooking as a school subject now.

Thank you for listening.

DIALOGUE

## 3 Choose a new subject

*Lösungsvorschlag:*

A: I'd like to learn Drama in school.

B: That's fun but other subjects are more important. I really want to learn more about technology.

A: I think we already know enough about technology and we can learn more when we're older. Also Technology is a hard subject.

B: Oh, I think Drama is harder than Technology. I don't like making presentations because everyone looks at you. And I don't want to be an actor.

A: That's why Drama is good! You learn how to speak in front of a lot of people.

B: I don't like speaking to an audience.

A: But you have to do it at school and later in your job.

B: OK, maybe we could do Drama once a week, but I don't want to act and sing or even dance for our parents, right?

A: Right! We just have fun together and people who enjoy it can act for an audience.

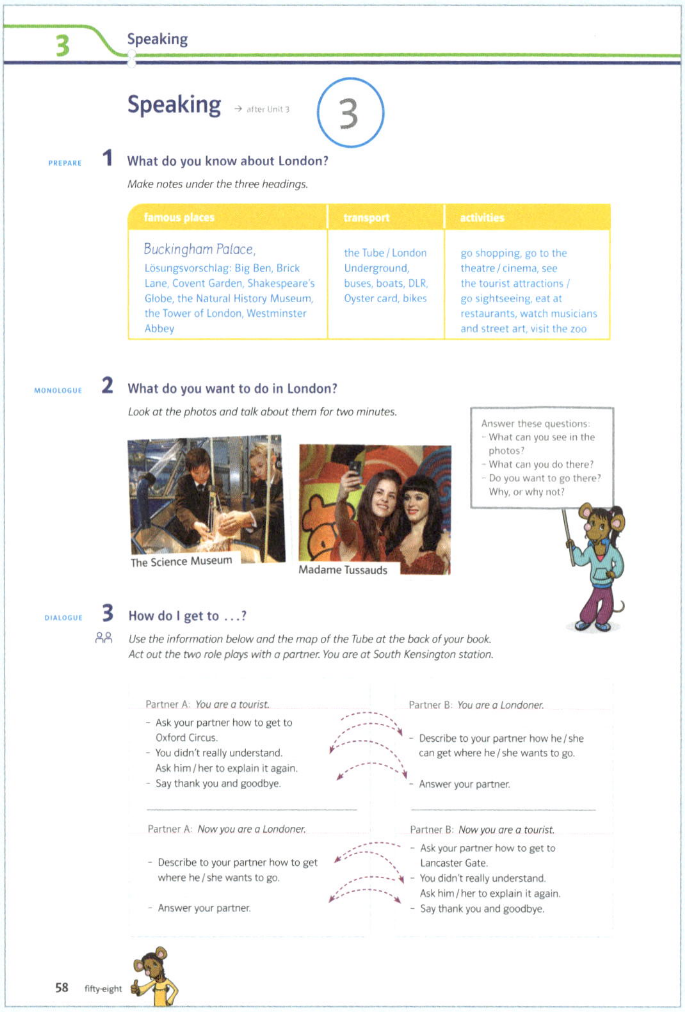
3 Speaking

## Speaking → after Unit 3 (3)

PREPARE **1 What do you know about London?**

*Make notes under the three headings.*

| famous places | transport | activities |
| --- | --- | --- |
| Buckingham Palace, Lösungsvorschlag: Big Ben, Brick Lane, Covent Garden, Shakespeare's Globe, the Natural History Museum, the Tower of London, Westminster Abbey | the Tube / London Underground, buses, boats, DLR, Oyster card, bikes | go shopping, go to the theatre / cinema, see the tourist attractions / go sightseeing, eat at restaurants, watch musicians and street art, visit the zoo |

MONOLOGUE **2 What do you want to do in London?**

*Look at the photos and talk about them for two minutes.*

The Science Museum

Madame Tussauds

Answer these questions:
- What can you see in the photos?
- What can you do there?
- Do you want to go there? Why, or why not?

DIALOGUE **3 How do I get to ...?**

*Use the information below and the map of the Tube at the back of your book. Act out the two role plays with a partner. You are at South Kensington station.*

Partner A: *You are a tourist.*
- Ask your partner how to get to Oxford Circus.
- You didn't really understand. Ask him / her to explain it again.
- Say thank you and goodbye.

Partner B: *You are a Londoner.*
- Describe to your partner how he / she can get where he / she wants to go.
- Answer your partner.

Partner A: *Now you are a Londoner.*
- Describe to your partner how to get where he / she wants to go.
- Answer your partner.

Partner B: *Now you are a tourist.*
- Ask your partner how to get to Lancaster Gate.
- You didn't really understand. Ask him / her to explain it again.
- Say thank you and goodbye.

58 fifty-eight

## Speaking → after Unit 3 (3)

MONOLOGUE

### 2 What do you want to do in London?

*Lösungsvorschläge:*

**The Science Museum**

In the first picture you can see the Science Museum. You can do lots of things there. You can find out more about science. And I think it's free.

I'd like to go there. The people are having fun. I like science and you can do things there which are interesting. I think that's exciting. It's free so you can go and see what it's like. You don't need to stay for a long time.

**Madame Tussauds**

In the other photo you can see Madame Tussauds. Somebody is standing next to a wax figure and is taking a photo. The figure looks very real. You can see lots of famous people there.

But you can also often see a long queue outside the museum. The tickets are expensive, I think.

I'd like to go to Madame Tussauds. My friend David went last year and said it was great. You see the people on the TV or in magazines, but it's different when you see the wax figures. They're not real, but they look real.

DIALOGUE

### 3 How do I get to ...?

*Lösungsvorschläge:*

**Role play 1**

A: Excuse me. Can you tell me the way to Oxford Circus? / How do I get to Oxford Circus, please?

B: Yes, take the Piccadilly line. Go north to Green Park and change onto the Victoria line. Go north again and Oxford Circus is the next stop.

A: I'm sorry. Can you say / explain that again, please? I didn't understand everything.

B: Yes, of course. Take the Piccadilly line. Go north to Green Park and change onto the Victoria line. Go north again. It's just one stop.

A: Thanks. Goodbye.

**Role play 2**

B: Excuse me. Can you tell me the way to Lancaster Gate, please?

A: Yes, of course. Take the Circle line and go west to Notting Hill Gate. Change onto the Central line. Go east and Lancaster Gate is the second stop.

B: I'm sorry. Can you say / explain that again, please? I didn't understand everything.

A: Yes, of course. Take the Circle line. Go west to Notting Hill Gate and change onto the Central line. Go east and Lancaster Gate is just two stops.

B: Thank you very much. Goodbye.

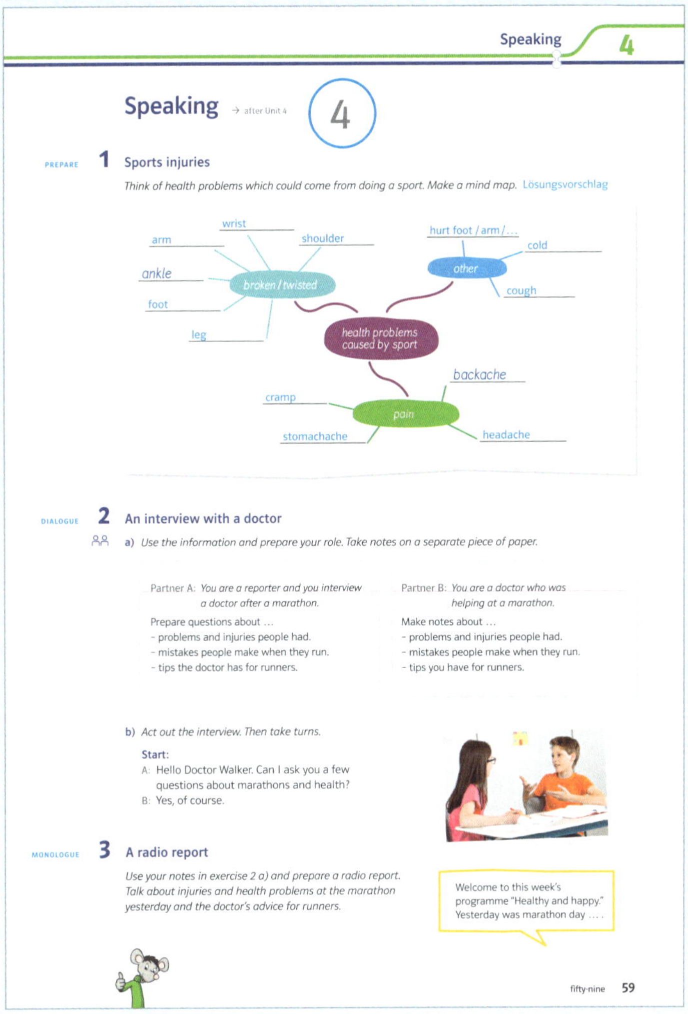



## Speaking → after Unit 4 ④

DIALOGUE

### 2 An interview with a doctor

a)

*Lösungsvorschläge:*

**Partner A**

- Were there many health problems / injuries?
- What mistakes do people make when they run?
- How should people train? What tips do you have?

**Partner B**

- twisted ankles, cramps, one broken arm
- don't have enough training or have too much training; run too fast too early; don't drink enough; wrong shoes
- good training plan, drink enough; good shoes

b)

*Lösungsvorschlag:*

A: Hello Doctor Walker. Can I ask you a few questions about marathons and health?
B: Yes, of course. There were some health problems at the marathon today.
A: Really? Were there many injuries?
B: Well, not so many, but one man fell and broke his arm. Then there were some twisted ankles and a lot of people got cramps.
A: Oh, are there always so many problems?
B: Yes, there are. But a broken arm doesn't happen very often. People often get cramps and a few people twist their ankles.
A: Why? What mistakes do people make?
B: A lot of people just don't train enough. And some people train too much.
A: But why is that a problem?
B: They are too tired on marathon day and not strong enough.
A: And what mistakes do people make when they run?
B: They run too fast too early and then they get a cramp. Or they don't drink enough – that's a big mistake.
A: So what advice / tips do you have? How should people train and how should they run?
B: They should make a good training plan and then follow the plan. They can talk to a sports doctor about the best plan for them. Oh, and they should wear good running shoes.
A: What other advice have you got for the race?
B: I've already said it before, but you must drink enough – before the race and during the race. It's so important.
A: Thank you very much for the interview.

MONOLOGUE

### 3 A radio report

*Lösungsvorschlag:*

Welcome to this week's programme "Healthy and happy."

Yesterday was marathon day and most people had a great time, but there were some health problems too. One man broke his arm during the race but the other injuries were not as serious. We spoke to Doctor Walker and she told us about some of the injuries and other problems that people often have when they run a marathon. She says that people often twist their ankles. Another problem is cramp. Doctor Walker says that people start running too fast too early. Then they get a cramp. Sometimes they are tired because they did too much training. Other people have not trained enough and that's a big problem too.

We asked Doctor Walker for advice for people who want to run a marathon. She said training is important, of course.

You have to make a training plan. Everybody needs a different plan and a sports doctor can help you with this.

You should always have good running shoes and you shouldn't wear new shoes on the day of the marathon.

One more tip: Make sure you drink enough – when you're training, before the marathon and while you are running the marathon. That's really important.

So, do you want to run a marathon? Well, you know what to do: Make a plan, buy good shoes and start training now!

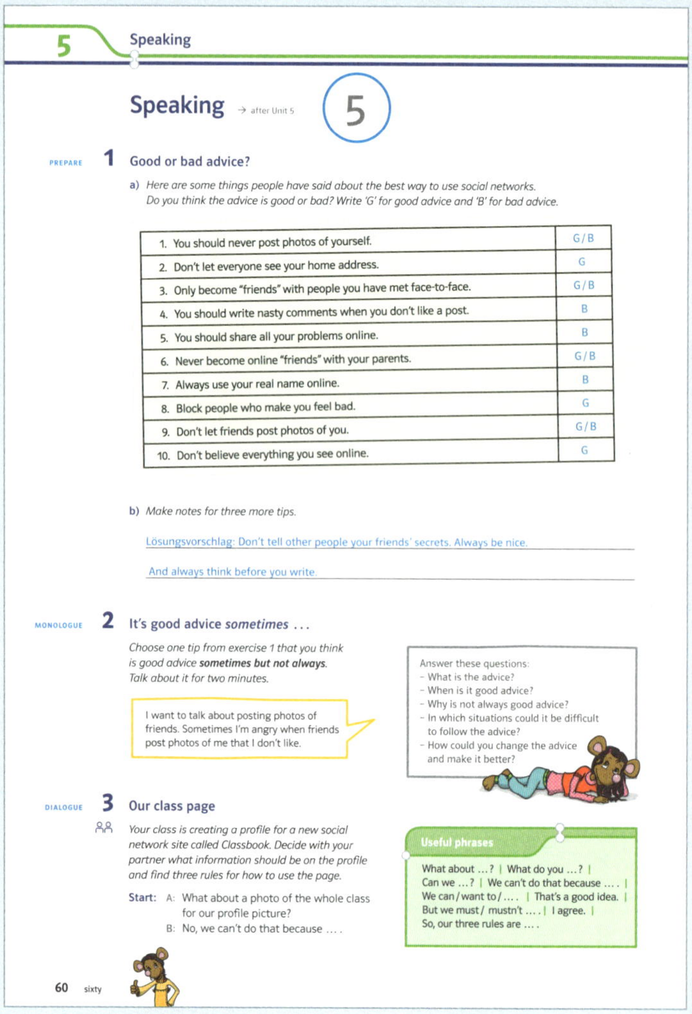
5 Speaking

## Speaking → after Unit 5 (5)

PREPARE **1 Good or bad advice?**

**a)** *Here are some things people have said about the best way to use social networks. Do you think the advice is good or bad? Write 'G' for good advice and 'B' for bad advice.*

| | |
|---|---|
| 1. You should never post photos of yourself. | G / B |
| 2. Don't let everyone see your home address. | G |
| 3. Only become "friends" with people you have met face-to-face. | G / B |
| 4. You should write nasty comments when you don't like a post. | B |
| 5. You should share all your problems online. | B |
| 6. Never become online "friends" with your parents. | G / B |
| 7. Always use your real name online. | B |
| 8. Block people who make you feel bad. | G |
| 9. Don't let friends post photos of you. | G / B |
| 10. Don't believe everything you see online. | G |

**b)** *Make notes for three more tips.*

Lösungsvorschlag: Don't tell other people your friends' secrets. Always be nice.

And always think before you write.

MONOLOGUE **2 It's good advice *sometimes* …**

*Choose one tip from exercise 1 that you think is good advice* ***sometimes but not always****. Talk about it for two minutes.*

I want to talk about posting photos of friends. Sometimes I'm angry when friends post photos of me that I don't like.

Answer these questions:
- What is the advice?
- When is it good advice?
- Why is not always good advice?
- In which situations could it be difficult to follow the advice?
- How could you change the advice and make it better?

DIALOGUE **3 Our class page**

*Your class is creating a profile for a new social network site called Classbook. Decide with your partner what information should be on the profile and find three rules for how to use the page.*

**Start:** A: What about a photo of the whole class for our profile picture?
B: No, we can't do that because … .

**Useful phrases**

What about …? | What do you …? | Can we …? | We can't do that because … . | We can / want to / … . | That's a good idea. | But we must / mustn't … . | I agree. | So, our three rules are … .

60 sixty

## Speaking → after Unit 5 (5)

MONOLOGUE

### 2 It's good advice *sometimes* …

*Lösungsvorschlag:*

I want to talk about posting photos of friends. Sometimes I'm angry when friends post photos of me that I don't like. But I really like it when someone takes a good photo of me and posts it online. It's always nice to see a good picture of yourself! I think the advice "Don't let friends post photos of you!" is OK when your friends are not close friends. It's not good advice for everybody. Maybe your friends just want to share happy moments with others. That's OK. It's also very hard to follow this advice. You can say, "Hey, never post pictures of me!", but people don't listen. Sometimes you don't know when you are in a picture online. I think better advice is "Check photos of yourself online." As soon as you see a photo that you don't like, tell the person who posted it. Or maybe you can block it yourself. That's best. And, of course, you shouldn't post awful pictures of other people!

DIALOGUE

### 3 Our class page

*Lösungsvorschlag:*

A: What about a photo of the whole class for our profile picture?

B: No, we can't do that because everyone can see the profile picture. Some parents don't want our photos online.

A: Oh, I'm sure that won't be a problem. Only people from our class can see it.

B: What do you mean only people from our class? We want to tell other people about our class too, don't we? So our online friends must be able to see everything on the page.

A: OK. Well, what about a photo of our school?

B: Yes, that's a good idea. And we can post information about what our class is doing at the moment: what projects we have and information about school trips, for example. But can we post information about what our classmates are doing outside of school? For example, if someone wins an award in sport or art.

A: Yes, we can. But we must ask them first.

B: I agree. So we have information about our class projects and our classmates on the page. And who can post information?

A: Everyone in the class. But they can only post nice things.

B: OK. Can we ask our classmates for help with homework?

A: Good idea. Er, or maybe not. Then we could ask one person to do the Maths homework and share the answers with everyone … We're not allowed to do that!

B: I agree. We can talk about homework, but we mustn't share answers.

A: So, our three rules for how to use the page are: Ask people before you post information about them. Always be nice. And don't post homework answers. OK?

B: OK!

## Checkliste Unit 1

| | üben am | erledigt und korrigiert am | erreichte Punktzahl | Übungen und Hinweise zum Wiederholen | nochmals üben am / bis |
|---|---|---|---|---|---|
| Test 1 | ______ | ______ | Ü1: ____ /5 | SB 168–169/Station 1 | ______ |
| | ______ | ______ | Ü2: ____ /5 | SB 168–169/Station 1 | ______ |
| | ______ | ______ | Ü3: ____ /5 | SB 11/3; SB 142–143/G1 | ______ |
| | ______ | ______ | Ü4: ____ /9 | SB 10/2; SB 11/4–5; SB 142–143/G1; WB 3–4/4–5 | ______ |
| Test 2 | ______ | ______ | Ü1: ____ /6 | SB 177/Jobs | ______ |
| | ______ | ______ | Ü2: ____ /5 | SB 169/Station 2 | ______ |
| | ______ | ______ | Ü3: ____ /4 | SB 13/10; SB 14/12; SB 143–145/G2; WB 5/8 | ______ |
| | ______ | ______ | Ü4: ____ /5 | SB 14/14; SB 143–145/G2; WB 6/10 | ______ |
| | ______ | ______ | Ü5: ____ /5 | SB 14/13; SB 145–146/G3; WB 5/9 | ______ |
| Test 3 | ______ | ______ | Ü1: ____ /8 | SB 170–171/Station 3 | ______ |
| | ______ | ______ | Ü2: ____ /6 | SB 16/19; SB 146–148/G4; SB 171/Comparing things; WB 8/14 | ______ |
| | ______ | ______ | Ü3: ____ /5 | SB 17/20; SB 146–148/G4; WB 8/14 | ______ |
| | ______ | ______ | Ü4: ____ /6 | SB 17/21–22; SB 148–149/G5; WB 8/15 | ______ |
| Class test 1 | ______ | ______ | Ü1: ____ /6 | SB 16/Text; WB 7/13 | ______ |
| | ______ | ______ | Ü2: ____ /12 | SB 12/7; SB 25/2; SB 142–143/G1; SB 145–146/G3 | ______ |
| | ______ | ______ | Ü3: ____ /7 | SB 10/Text | ______ |
| Class test 2 | ______ | ______ | Ü1: ____ /7 | SB 16/Text; WB 3/3 | ______ |
| | ______ | ______ | Ü2: ____ /6 | SB 10/Text | ______ |
| | ______ | ______ | Ü3: ____ /14 | SB 17/20; SB 148–149/G5 | ______ |

SB 168–169/Station 1 = Schülerbuch Seite 168 und 169, Vokabular zu Station 1
SB 177/Jobs = Schülerbuch Seite 177, Abschnitt zu *„Jobs"*
SB 142–143/G1 = Schülerbuch Seite 142 und 143, Grammatikkapitel 1
SB 11/3 = Schülerbuch Seite 11, Übung 3
WB 3–4/4–5 = Workbook Seite 3 und 4, Übungen 4 und 5

## Checkliste Unit 2

| | üben am | erledigt und korrigiert am | erreichte Punktzahl | Übungen und Hinweise zum Wiederholen | nochmals üben am / bis |
|---|---|---|---|---|---|
| Test 1 | | | Ü1: ___ /7 | SB 174–175/Station 1 | |
| | | | Ü2: ___ /5 | SB 32/8; SB 175/Subjects at school; WB 16/1–2 | |
| | | | Ü3: ___ /4 | SB 30/Text; SB 174–175/Station 1 | |
| | | | Ü4: ___ /5 | SB 31/3; SB 149–151/G6; WB 17/3 | |
| | | | Ü5: ___ /4 | SB 31/4–5; SB 149–151/G6; WB 18/5 | |
| Test 2 | | | Ü1: ___ /5 | SB 33/Text; SB 176–177/Station 2 | |
| | | | Ü2: ___ /6 | SB 176–177/Station 2 | |
| | | | Ü3: ___ /5 | SB 34/10; SB 151–152/G7; WB 19/7c | |
| | | | Ü4: ___ /5 | SB 151–152/G7; WB 20/9 | |
| | | | Ü5: ___ /4 | SB 34/10; SB 142–143/G1; SB 151–152/G7 | |
| Class test 1 | | | Ü1: ___ /6 | WB 17/3 | |
| | | | Ü2: ___ /6 | SB 40–41/Text | |
| | | | Ü3: ___ /14 | SB 34/12; WB 16/1–2; WB 20/10 | |
| Class test 2 | | | Ü1: ___ /7 | WB 19/7a–b | |
| | | | Ü2: ___ /12 | SB 40–41/Text | |
| | | | Ü3: ___ /12 | SB 29/3; SB 142–143/G1; SB 145–146/G3 | |

## Checkliste Unit 3

| | üben am | erledigt und korrigiert am | erreichte Punktzahl | Übungen und Hinweise zum Wiederholen | nochmals üben am / bis |
|---|---|---|---|---|---|
| Test 1 | | | Ü1: ___ /4 | SB 51/4; SB 181–182/Station 1; WB 31/1 | |
| | | | Ü2: ___ /4 | SB 51/4; SB 181–182/Station 1; WB 31/2 | |
| | | | Ü3: ___ /4 | SB 181–182/Station 1; WB 34/7 | |
| | | | Ü4: ___ /6 | SB 52/2; SB 53/4; SB 153–154/G8; WB 32/3 | |
| | | | Ü5: ___ /7 | SB 52/3; SB 153–154/G8; WB 32–33/4–5 | |
| Test 2 | | | Ü1: ___ /7 | SB 46/2; SB 142–143/G1; SB 239–240/Irregular verbs | |
| | | | Ü2: ___ /3 | SB 54/Text; SB 182/Station 2 | |
| | | | Ü3: ___ /6 | SB 55/9; SB 154–156/G9 | |
| | | | Ü4: ___ /7 | SB 55/10; SB 154–156/G9; WB 35/9 | |
| Test 3 | | | Ü1: ___ /5 | SB 56/Text; SB 182–183/Station 3 | |
| | | | Ü2: ___ /5 | SB 57/14–16; SB 156–157/G10; WB 37/15 | |
| | | | Ü3: ___ /9 | SB 57/14–16; SB 65/3; SB 156–157/G10; WB 36/14 | |
| | | | Ü4: ___ /5 | SB 157–158/G11 | |
| Class test 1 | | | Ü1: ___ /6 | WB 31/1 | |
| | | | Ü2: ___ /6 | SB 62–63/Story; WB 39/21 | |
| | | | Ü3: ___ /18 | WB 37/17 | |
| Class test 2 | | | Ü1: ___ /8 | SB 51/3; SB 53/6; WB 34/7–8 | |
| | | | Ü2: ___ /6 | SB 62–63/Story; WB 39/21 | |
| | | | Ü3: ___ /28 | SB 64/4 | |

## Checkliste Unit 4

| | üben am | erledigt und korrigiert am | erreichte Punktzahl | Übungen und Hinweise zum Wiederholen | nochmals üben am / bis |
|---|---|---|---|---|---|
| Test 1 | ______ | ______ | Ü1: ___ /6 | SB 188/Parts of the body | ______ |
| | ______ | ______ | Ü2: ___ /7 | SB 187–188/Check-in, Station 1 | ______ |
| | ______ | ______ | Ü3: ___ /6 | SB 71/2–3; SB 158–160/G12; WB 46/4 | ______ |
| | ______ | ______ | Ü4: ___ /4 | SB 71/2–3; WB 46/4 | ______ |
| Test 2 | ______ | ______ | Ü1: ___ /4 | SB 73/8; SB 190/Health | ______ |
| | ______ | ______ | Ü2: ___ /7 | SB 73/8; SB 190/Health | ______ |
| | ______ | ______ | Ü3: ___ /4 | SB 72/6; SB 158–160/G12; WB 48/9 | ______ |
| | ______ | ______ | Ü4: ___ /9 | SB 73/7; SB 158–160/G12; WB 48/9 | ______ |
| Test 3 | ______ | ______ | Ü1: ___ /6 | SB 190/Station 3 | ______ |
| | ______ | ______ | Ü2: ___ /8 | SB 74/11; WB 51/14 | ______ |
| | ______ | ______ | Ü3: ___ /6 | SB 75/12; SB 158–160/G12 | ______ |
| | ______ | ______ | Ü4: ___ /5 | SB 75/13; SB 83/3; SB 158–160/G12; WB 51/15 | ______ |
| Class test 1 | ______ | ______ | Ü1: ___ /6 | SB 74/Text; WB 46/3; WB 50/13 | ______ |
| | ______ | ______ | Ü2: ___ /8 | SB 74/Text | ______ |
| | ______ | ______ | Ü3: ___ /20 | SB 69/4; SB 75/13; WB 47/5; WB 51/16 | ______ |
| Class test 2 | ______ | ______ | Ü1: ___ /10 | SB 72/Text; SB 73/8; WB 48/8 | ______ |
| | ______ | ______ | Ü2: ___ /5 | SB 80–81/Story; WB 56/26 | ______ |
| | ______ | ______ | Ü3: ___ /12 | SB 73/9; WB 49/11 | ______ |

## Checkliste Unit 5

| | üben am | erledigt und korrigiert am | erreichte Punktzahl | Übungen und Hinweise zum Wiederholen | nochmals üben am / bis |
|---|---|---|---|---|---|
| Test 1 | ______ | ______ | Ü1: ___ /5 | SB 90/2; SB 195/Media collocations; WB 62/1 | ______ |
| | ______ | ______ | Ü2: ___ /8 | SB 195–196/Station 1 | ______ |
| | ______ | ______ | Ü3: ___ /3 | SB 93/4; WB 63/5; WB 68/17 | ______ |
| | ______ | ______ | Ü4: ___ /5 | SB 93/2; SB 161–162/G13; WB 63/5 | ______ |
| | ______ | ______ | Ü5: ___ /4 | SB 94/5; SB 162–164/G14; WB 64/8 | ______ |
| Test 2 | ______ | ______ | Ü1: ___ /7 | SB 197–198/Station 2 | ______ |
| | ______ | ______ | Ü2: ___ /4 | SB 96/9; SB 164–165/G15 | ______ |
| | ______ | ______ | Ü3: ___ /6 | SB 96/10; SB 164–165/G15; WB 65/10 | ______ |
| | ______ | ______ | Ü4: ___ /5 | SB 96/11; SB 165/G16 | ______ |
| Class test 1 | ______ | ______ | Ü1: ___ /6 | – | ______ |
| | ______ | ______ | Ü2: ___ /5 | SB 92/Text | ______ |
| | ______ | ______ | Ü3: ___ /18 | SB 93/3; SB 104/2; WB 66/12 | ______ |
| Class test 2 | ______ | ______ | Ü1: ___ /6 | SB 95/Text; SB 105/1; WB 65/9 | ______ |
| | ______ | ______ | Ü2: ___ /4 | SB 92/Text | ______ |
| | ______ | ______ | Ü3: ___ /14 | WB 66/11 | ______ |

2

Green Line G9

Fit für Tests und Klassenarbeiten Lösungsheft

LANGUAGE

## 3 A true story!

*Put in the missing words in the correct **adjective** or **adverb** form.*

careful dirty good happy hard hungry large new safe

Harrods once sold lions in their shop in London. In 1969 two Australians[1] who lived in London bought one and took it home to their flat. They called it Christian. Lions aren't ________________ animals and they can live ________________ in a flat. Christian liked to play and the two men played with him. Even as a young lion he bit ________________ while he was playing, but the two men always played ________________ and they still have all their fingers! Lions are usually dangerous, but the men believed that Christian was ________________ and they walked him in Hyde Park. But they were always careful and made sure that he was not ________________ when they went out.

When he was one year old Christian was already a ________________ lion and the Australians decided that London was not a good place for him any more. So they took him to Africa and some animal experts helped him to live alone. Christian learnt ________________ and a few years later, when the Australians visited him in his ________________ home, he already had his own family.

_____ /9

LANGUAGE

## 4 How do they do it?

*The friends do things differently. Complete the sentences with the correct **comparative forms**.*

Underline the adjective in the first sentence before you complete the second sentence.

1. Jay is a beautiful singer.
   He sings more beautifully than Luke.
2. Dave thinks most computer games are too easy.
   He beats the computer ________________________ his friends.
3. Holly isn't a good swimmer. She can't swim ________________________ her friends.
4. Luke is a good football player. He plays football ________________________ Dave.
5. Olivia likes loud music. She plays her music ________________________ her sister Lucy.
6. Olivia is a fast reader. She reads books ________________________ Holly.

_____ /5

1 Australian [ɒs'treɪliən] Australier/in

_____ /24

# Class test 1 → after Unit 3

VIEWING

## 1 London life

*Luke and his cousin are in central London. Watch the film and tick ✔ the correct answer.*

1. Luke and his cousin went …
   a) ☐ by bike.
   b) ☐ by boat.
   c) ☐ on a coach trip.

2. Big Ben has …
   a) ☐ 334 steps.
   b) ☐ 342 steps.
   c) ☐ 433 steps.

3. The people who built the London Eye came from …
   a) ☐ China and Pakistan.
   b) ☐ Germany and France.
   c) ☐ Poland and Canada.

4. They built Shakespeare's Globe in …
   a) ☐ 1799.
   b) ☐ 1979.
   c) ☐ 1997.

5. William Shakespeare came to London …
   a) ☐ 140 years ago.
   b) ☐ 400 years ago.
   c) ☐ 1,400 years ago.

6. The Tower of London is about …
   a) ☐ 150 years old.
   b) ☐ 415 years old.
   c) ☐ 950 years old.

_____ /6

READING

## 2 Information from a website

*Read the website. Take notes and answer the questions. If you can't find the answer in the text, write down the name of the link where you can find the information.*

Home | Where to find us | Special tours | Buy tickets online | What people say about us

### THAMES BOAT TOURS

On our amazing tours you can see Big Ben, the London Eye, St Paul's, the Tower of London, Tower Bridge and many more of London's most famous tourist attractions. In good or bad weather you can enjoy your trip on our comfortable boats with toilets and a café which sells drinks and snacks.

**Boat tour times:** May – September: 9 a.m. to 5:30 p.m., every 30 minutes
October – March: 9 a.m. to 4 p.m., every 30 minutes
Open 7 days a week (closed 25th December). Tours take 45 – 50 minutes.

**Tickets:** Tickets cost £15 (£14) for an adult and £8.50 (£7.50) for a child.
Buy tickets on the boat or online (online prices in red).

1. How often do the boat tours go? ______________________
2. Where do the tours start? ______________________
3. What time is the first tour of the day? ______________________
4. What days can you go on a boat tour? ______________________
5. Where can you buy the tickets? ______________________
6. How much are the tickets for two adults and two children? ______________________

_____ /6

MEDIATION

## 3 The Shakespeare's Globe tour

*You are in London on a tour of Shakespeare's Globe with your family. Your English is better than your parents'. Tell them what the tour guide said.*

"Hello and welcome to my tour of the world of William Shakespeare. First let me take you back to the year 1592 because it was in this year that Shakespeare first came to London. He was 25 years old when he left his wife and two children at home in Stratford-upon-Avon and went to live in London to make some money with his plays.

Remember what life was like in this time – there were no computer games, no TVs, no radios and no phones! So what did people do in the evening? They went to the theatre! Shakespeare's plays were already popular when he came to London and when he and his team built this theatre seven years later. They soon had audiences of three thousand. People who did not have much money also came here. They paid just one penny and stood here in the middle of the theatre. Others paid more and sat more comfortably.

Try to imagine what it was like. Not like our theatres today – the audience was loud and rude. They didn't sit politely and they laughed loudly too. And they threw things at the actors when they didn't like the play!

Shakespeare's plays were more popular than musicals today. They were funny and scary and exciting. Some people say that his plays were too good and they don't believe that he wrote them all. He was young when he came to London and he wrote a lot of plays and poems very quickly. How did he do it? Some people think that other people wrote Shakespeare's plays. They're not right if you ask me!"

*Also er sagt, dass Shakespeare 1592 nach London kam.*

______________________________________________

______________________________________________

______________________________________________

______________________________________________

______________________________________________

______________________________________________

______________________________________________

______________________________________________

______________________________________________

______________________________________________

______________________________________________

____/18

____/30

# Class test 2

→ after Unit 3

LISTENING

## 1 Where do they want to go?

5 ◎ **a)** *Listen to the four dialogues. Fill in the grid where the people want to go.*

| They want to go to … | They get on the Tube at … | They get off the Tube at … |
|---|---|---|
| 1. | St. Paul's | |
| 2. | Moorgate | |
| 3. | Charing Cross | |
| 4. | Oxford Circus | |

**b)** *Look at the map of the Tube at the back of your book and find the four Tube stations. Listen again and follow the routes on the map. Fill in at which station each person needs to get off the Tube.*

_____ /8

READING

## 2 Welcome to the London Aquarium!

*Read the text. Are the statements true or false? Tick ✔ the correct answer.*

The London Aquarium is one of London's most popular attractions and one of Europe's largest collections of fish and sea life. We are only a minute away from the London Eye so you can easily visit us on a day out to the city centre. But make sure you plan enough time! There are a lot of things to do here.

Find out about many different kinds of fish and sea life here. Which fish is the most dangerous? Which one swims fastest? What do they eat? You can also give food to the fish yourself. And are you brave enough to walk through a tunnel while sharks swim around you? One of the favourite attractions at the aquarium is our open pool full of rays. Put your fingers in the water and move them quickly and the fish come to you. What do the fish feel like? Come and find out!

If you want to have an extra special day, you can do a 'behind-the-scenes' tour and find out how we look after our animals. Or you can swim with the sharks! Of course, that costs extra and you must get your ticket a few days before.

| | true | false |
|---|---|---|
| 1. The London Aquarium has more fish than all other aquariums in Europe. | ☐ | ☐ |
| 2. You can walk there from the London Eye. | ☐ | ☐ |
| 3. You can give the fish some food. | ☐ | ☐ |
| 4. The sharks swim in a tunnel. | ☐ | ☐ |
| 5. You can feel some of the fish. | ☐ | ☐ |
| 6. If you pay more, you can swim with some fish in the aquarium. | ☐ | ☐ |

_____ /6

LANGUAGE

## 3 A famous father

*Complete the dialogue with the verbs in the **present perfect simple** or use short answers.*

be | break | lose | play | watch✔ | win

Rory: Have ______ you ever watched ______ a sports event in a stadium?

Tara: Yes, I ______ . My father plays rugby. He's really famous in the world of sports! So I ______ to a lot of rugby matches. Dad ______ never ______ a game with me in the stadium.

Rory: Wow! And ______ your father ______ any important prizes?

Tara: Yes, his team won the Prince George Cup ten years ago.

Rory: And what about you? ______ you ever ______ rugby? It's not really a girls' sport …

Tara: Hey! Women's rugby is great! But I know lots of girls who ______ an arm or leg in rugby matches. It's not my thing. I love hockey.

Rory: But that's even *more* dangerous!

______ /6

LANGUAGE

## 4 What has happened?

*Answer the questions with the correct words. Use the **present perfect simple**.*

she – win – a race | you – not do – your homework – yet | he – break – his arm | our team – not score – any goals – yet✔ | I – just – run – in a marathon

1. Why are you all so angry? – Our team hasn't scored any goals yet.
2. Why are you so tired? – ______
3. Why is Lisa proud? – ______
4. Why is Carl going to hospital? – ______
5. Why can't I play tennis now? – ______

______ /4

______ /23

# Test 2

→ after Station 2

VOCABULARY

## 1 I don't feel well …

*Look at the pictures and read what these people think. Complete the sentences.*

My head hurts.

1 She's got a ________________.

I've got a bad pain.

2 He's got a ________________.

I fell over.

3 She has ____________ her leg.

I can't eat anything.

4 He feels ________________.

____ /4

VOCABULARY

## 2 A bad day

*Complete the missing words.*

I've had a bad day. I've _ _ _ _ _ _ _ my ankle!

Oh no! Have you seen the _ _ _ _ _ _?

Yes. She gave me some _ _ _ _ _ _ _ _ to put on the ankle. It stops the pain.

I've had a bad day too. I've got a cough. I think I've caught a _ _ _ _.

Do you have a _ _ _ _ _? Get a _ _ _ _ _ _ _ _ _ _ _ _ from the doctor and then go to bed.

I never take _ _ _ _ _.

But sometimes they really help.

____ /7

LANGUAGE

## 3 An accident

*Underline the correct words: **just** or **yet**.*

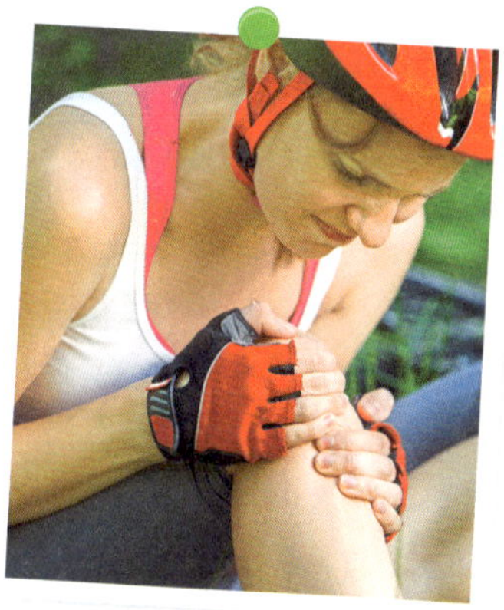

"I've **just / yet** fallen off my bike. I can feel a pain in my leg, but I haven't looked at it **just / yet**. Maybe it's broken! I don't know. The accident has **just / yet** happened and I haven't been to the doctor **just / yet**."

_____ /4

LANGUAGE

## 4 The runner's morning

*Look at the pictures and the words. Write a question and an answer for each picture.*

1. have – breakfast

Has he had breakfast yet?

get up

– No, he hasn't. He's just got up.

2. go – stadium

______________________________

say – goodbye to his mum

______________________________

3. race – finish

______________________________

runners – start

______________________________

4. win – race

______________________________

race – not finish

______________________________

_____ /9

_____ /24

# Test 3

→ after Station 3

VOCABULARY

## 1 Advice for Gwen

*Complete the e-mail to Gwen. There are three extra words.*

almost | award | cold | cramp | like | Player | runner | should | shouldn't

Dear Gwen,

I've heard you're running in the marathon trials. That's great!

I've never run in a marathon, but I play football. Last year my team had an important match. I wanted to win the ______________ for 'Best ______________'. I started really well, but then I got a ______________ . It really hurt. I ______________ had to leave the match! Do you know what it's ______________? Well, it's awful and you ______________ always warm up for a match or for a run, believe me.

See you soon!

Sam

_____ /6

LANGUAGE

## 2 Signal words

*Put the words in the grid.*

after that ✔ | before | ever | in 1998 | just | last week | two weeks ago | yesterday | yet

| You often use it with the simple past: | You often use it with the present perfect simple: |
|---|---|
| – after that | ______________ |
| ______________ | ______________ |
| ______________ | ______________ |
| ______________ | ______________ |
| ______________ | ______________ |

_____ /8

The signal words for the **simple past** are usually for an action that started and finished in the past.
The signal words for the **present perfect simple** often show a link to the present.

LANGUAGE

## 3 An interview with Jay

*Underline the correct form of the verbs.*

Diana: **Have / Did** you ever run in a race, Jay?

Jay: Me? No, I **'ve never run / never ran** in a race.

Diana: And **have you ever won / did you ever win** a sports award?

Jay: No, sports are not really my thing, but I **won / have won** a dance prize last year.

Diana: Ah! Which prize **did you win / have you won**?

Jay: It **was / has been** the 'Greenwich Young Dancer' award. I'm really proud of it!

_____ /6

LANGUAGE

## 4 A real marathon

*Ayla is now 18 and she ran her first full marathon yesterday. Put in the correct form of the verbs. Use the* ***simple past*** *or* ***present perfect simple****.*

never have ✔ | run ✔ | never be | feel | say | never see | be

2nd

I have never had as much fun as I had yesterday. I ran in a real marathon for the first time!

Of course, it was very, very hard. I _____ _____ so tired, but it was amazing.

Yesterday evening I _____ so good.

My mother _____, "I _____ a girl who looks as happy as you."

She _____ right!

_____ /5

_____ /25

# Class test 1 → after Unit 4

LISTENING

## 1 At the stadium

6 ⊙ *Steven is a young football player who has just finished his first big match. Listen to the interview with a reporter and answer the questions. Write 1 to 3 words.*

1. Has Steven had a lot of moments like this one before? ______________________
2. Does he think he is the best player on the team? ______________________
3. When the match started, was Steven scared? ______________________
4. Where did Steven's father watch the match? ______________________
5. Who has always believed in him? ______________________
6. What is he going to do at nine o'clock this evening? ______________________

_____ /6

READING

## 2 The marathon website

a) *Read the website. Match the correct headings to the text. There are two extra headings.*

A How healthy must I be?
B What's the best way to start training?
C Who can run?
D When is the half marathon?
E Are there any other tips?
F Where can I get good running shoes?
G Should I stop training if my legs or ankles hurt?

Run&Fun

Home | About | News | Where and when | Advice

[C] 1. Adults of 18 or older can run in the full marathon. Anybody of 12 years or older can run in the half marathon.

[ ] 2. You must get fit before you run a long distance. A marathon is hard, and you should talk to your doctor about it first. A half marathon is hard too, but if you start with the training now, you can do it!

[ ] 3. Start slowly. You should run often but not for too long. Four days a week for 30 minutes is a good way to start. Do you think that 30 minutes' running is too hard? Then walk – that's training too. Start running when you feel ready.

[ ] 4. Yes, stop right away! Maybe it is not a big problem, but you should see your doctor and find out. Never run when your legs or ankles hurt. You can make a small problem into a big problem fast.

[ ] 5. Wear good running shoes. In the marathon, use the shoes that you always wear for training. You should never wear new shoes on the day of the race.

_____ /4

**b)** *Look at the website on page 44 again. Are the statements true or false? Tick ✔ the correct answer. Which lines in the text tell you that the statements are true or false?*

| | true | false | line(s) |
|---|---|---|---|
| 1. Only adults can run in the full marathon. | ✔ | ☐ | 1 |
| 2. You should not run every day when you start training. | ☐ | ☐ | |
| 3. You must run – walking does not help in training. | ☐ | ☐ | |
| 4. Running can make a small injury worse. | ☐ | ☐ | |
| 5. You should buy new running shoes the day before the marathon. | ☐ | ☐ | |

_____/4

WRITING

## 3 The match

*Holly has some questions about a match you have just played in. It can be a football, rugby or basketball match, or any other team sport. Write an e-mail to Holly and answer her questions.*

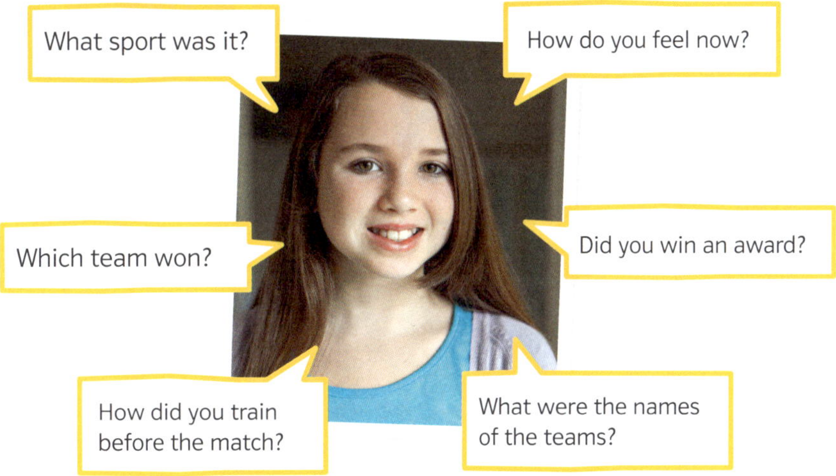


Dear Holly,

______________________________________________

______________________________________________

______________________________________________

______________________________________________

______________________________________________

______________________________________________

______________________________________________

______________________________________________

______________________________________________

______________________________________________

_____/20

_____/34

# Class test 2 → after Unit 4

LISTENING

## 1 At the doctor's

7 a) *Listen and put the pictures in the order they really happened. There is one extra picture.*

A ☐

B ☐

C ☐

D ☐

E ☐

F 1

____ /4

b) *Listen again and fill in the grid.*

| | Tara | Rory | Mr West |
|---|---|---|---|
| 1. Who had a sports accident? | ☐ | ☐ | ☐ |
| 2. Who hurt his or her hand? | ☐ | ☐ | ☐ |
| 3. Who has used ointment? | ☐ | ☐ | ☐ |
| 4. Who has got a pain? | ☐ | ☐ | ☐ |

____ /6

READING

## 2 The best

*Read the article. Copy 1–10 words from the text to show that the the statements on page 47 are correct.*

### We're the best!

Now everybody knows: Our school is the very best! Well, we're the best at football! Last Sunday eight schools played in four exciting matches. Redhill School played against Lewis School, and did we win? Yes, we did: seven to one – what a score! And who won the award for 'Best Player'? – Tim, of course. Four of the seven goals were his. Tim, we're proud of you!

But the day wasn't perfect. Jimmy Waters twisted his ankle while he was trying to stop a goal. That evening, while the other team members were having a party and telling stories about the great match, Jimmy was at home in bed. Sorry, Jimmy! You were doing a great job when you twisted your ankle, and a party is always better when you are there. Next time!

The other thing that went wrong was very funny. One of the Newpark School players has got a 5-year-old sister whose name is Maria. She loves watching football and playing it. In the middle of the match she ran onto the pitch, caught the ball and kicked it into the goal! Fantastic, Maria – your goal was the best thing that happened on a great day!

1. Each school team played one match. *eight schools played in four exciting matches*
2. Tim's award is not a surprise. ______
3. Jimmy hurt his foot. ______
4. Jimmy didn't go to the party. ______
5. Maria is a football fan. ______
6. The fans loved Maria's goal. ______

____/5

MEDIATION

## 3 At the surgery

*Your Welsh friend Jenny is staying with you for a week. Today Jenny is sick and you take her to the doctor's. Tell Jenny what the doctor says in English and tell the doctor what Jenny says in German.*

Don't tell Jenny every detail the doctor says. Just ask her questions and give the doctor's advice.

You: Meine Freundin fühlt sich krank.

Doctor: Frage sie bitte, ob sie etwas Schlechtes gegessen hat.

You: *Have you eaten anything bad?*

Jenny: Well, I've eaten the same as you, but you aren't sick.

You: ______

Doctor: Hat sie Fieber?

You: ______

Jenny: No, I haven't. I feel cold.

You: ______

Doctor: Bitte sie, den Mund aufzumachen.

You: ______

Doctor: Oh, alles rot. Offensichtlich hat sie eine schlimme Erkältung.

You: ______

Doctor: Sie sollte viel trinken und am besten im Bett bleiben bis sie sich wieder besser fühlt.

You: ______

Jenny: OK. Thanks for your help.

____/12

____/27

# Unit 5 Stay in touch

## Test 1

→ after Station 1

VOCABULARY

### 1 Texts, e-mails, profiles …

*Match the sentence parts. Draw lines.*

| | |
|---|---|
| 1. I text … | a) about 20 texts every day. |
| 2. I receive … | b) her e-mails about ten times every day! |
| 3. On social networks I change … | c) photos of my friends after a party. |
| 4. I always post … | d) my best friend every morning. |
| 5. My brother plays … | e) my profile very often. |
| 6. And my mum checks … | f) video games all day. |

_____ /5

VOCABULARY

### 2 Tell Kate

*Put in the missing words. There are two extra words.*

agony | as soon as | care | face-to-face | forever | friendship | site | social | teen | worry

"I'm Kate – I'm an ________________ aunt and I work for a ________________ magazine. People write to me and tell me their problems. For young people, ________________ is very important and most questions are about problems with friends. I don't think that ________________ networks make teenagers' lives easier. They see photos online of friends who are having fun and they ________________ that they aren't part of the group. But you shouldn't believe everything you see online. The problems often go away ________________ people talk to each other ________________. Most people ________________ about their friends and they want to help. So talk to your friends!"

_____ /8

VOCABULARY

## 3 What's your advice?

*Tara is talking to her friends about their problems. Use the words and show understanding or give advice.*

1. Lisa: I'm so sad. My best friend is going to live in Canada.
   Tara: ____________________ sorry – feel – upset
2. Rory: One of my classmates often posts awful pictures of me.
   Tara: ____________________ my advice – talk to him
3. Anne: I feel so alone with my problems.
   Tara: ____________________ why – not ask – friends for help

____/3

LANGUAGE

## 4 Kate's advice

*Underline the correct words.*

**This is my advice for teens who use social networks:**

- Don't start to worry **whenever / before** you see a photo of friends who are laughing without you. It's just a picture of one moment.
- **Because / Before** you make a person an online friend, make sure you know who he or she is.
- Block a person **as soon as / until** you have a bad feeling about them.
- Be extra careful when you post photos of yourself and others **because / after** you don't always know who sees them.
- Don't act **until / like** you are too crazy or silly online. Not everybody knows you in real life!

____/5

LANGUAGE

## 5 Carl doesn't have a girlfriend, does he?

*Complete the dialogue with the correct **question tags**.*

Anne: Hello. You're Carl, aren't you ?

Carl: Yes, I am. But I don't know you, ____________ ?

Anne: I'm Anne Rees.

Carl: Oh, Anne! My sister is your partner at the Tennis Club, ____________ ?

Anne: Yes, she is. She has told me a lot about you. You've just won the prize for the 'Best School Blog', ____________ ? Fantastic! And you don't have a girlfriend, ____________ ?

Carl: Uh … no, I don't. Why?

____/4

____/25

# Test 2 → after Station 2

VOCABULARY

## 1 The broken bike

*Complete the missing words.*

**Olivia says** 12:15 p.m. 3rd April

I'm going c _ _ _ _! My bike is broken again and I can't _ i _ it. I've done it a _ _ l _ _ _ _ times before, but this time I don't understand it.

| | |
|---|---|
| **Dave** 12:20 p.m. | What on _ _ _ _ h is the problem? |
| **Olivia** 12:22 p.m. | The wheels don't move. |
| **Holly** 12:24 p.m. | Look for s _ _ _ - b _ - _ _ _ p advice online. Or _ _ i _ George (he can always help). |
| **Dave** 12:30 p.m. | Who's George? I'm a g _ _ _ _ _ and I can come to your house right away! |

_____ /7

LANGUAGE

## 2 I'm not allowed to …

*Look at the photos. Complete the text with the correct form of* ***not be able to*** *or* ***not be allowed to****.*

"My dad ______________ use his new smartphone very well. I could help him, but he doesn't want my help."

"Once my phone was broken and I ______________ chat with my friends. I felt awful!"

"I ______________ use our computer at home after 8 p.m."

"My sister has got a tablet, but I ______________ go anywhere near it."

_____ /4

LANGUAGE

## 3 Technology and my family

*Complete the sentences with the correct form of* ***be able to****,* ***be allowed to*** *or* ***have to****.*
*Use the simple present or simple past.*

Look at the sentences and decide if you need to use "be allowed to" (= *dürfen*), "be able to" (= *können*) or "have to" (= *müssen*). Be careful: Sometimes you have to use the negative form!

1. I ______________________________ have my first smartphone this year. My parents have said yes at last!
   I ______________________________ have one last year because Mum said I was too young.
2. My sister ______________________________ use a computer when she was six. It was easy!
   She ______________________________ play video games on the computer very well now.
3. My brother and I ______________________________ ask our parents when we want to use the computer. We just use it.
   We ______________________________ ask when we were younger because we didn't know how to turn it on.

______ /6

LANGUAGE

## 4 A new phone

*Cross out the wrong words.*

Ben: My new phone was very expensive. What if I lose it?
Paul: You **could / should / shouldn't** worry so much!
Ben: You're right. Hey, I'm bored. Let's go swimming.
Paul: Oh, sorry. I **'m allowed to / have to / 'm able to** go home soon. I don't have much time.
You **could / shouldn't / are able to** ask Rory.
He has time today.
Ben: Rory? Oh, … no. I can go alone.
Paul: Alone? Really? Well, don't take your new phone with you.
Ben: Why **aren't able to / shouldn't / don't have to** I take my phone with me?
Paul: You **could / should / have to** lose it!

______ /5

______ /22

# Class test 1 → after Unit 5

VIEWING

## 1 In the news

*Watch the film. Put the sentences in the correct order. Write the numbers (1–6) in the boxes.*

☐ **A** A young woman was on the bus when she heard about the new game.

☐ **B** A reporter explains why people are standing in a queue.

☐ **C** The reporter may try the game.

☐ **D** A young man found out about the game when he was reading the newspaper.

☐ **E** Holly texted Olivia about the new 'Fantasia' game.

☐ **F** The reporter starts talking to Olivia.

_____ /6

READING

## 2 Thanks Kate

*Read Lenny's letter to the magazine* TeenSpeak. *Copy 1–10 words from the text to show that the statements on page 53 are correct.*

Dear *TeenSpeak*,

I want to say thank you to agony aunt Kate because she really helped me.

I was spending too much time alone with my smartphone and when I saw photos of my classmates who were having fun without me, I felt sad. People at school like me and say I'm clever, but they don't invite me to do things with them.

One day I saw a photo online of my classmates Jeff, Pam and Manisha. They were enjoying themselves at the boating lake. I love boats, but they are no fun alone. The photo was too much, so I wrote to Kate.

"Talk to them face-to-face," replied Kate. "Just tell them that you would like to go too. And remember: Everybody looks happy in the photos they post online but that doesn't mean they are having fun all the time."

I sit next to Jeff in History lessons so it wasn't difficult to talk to him. The next time I saw some happy boating lake photos I said, "Hey, did you have fun at the lake yesterday? You know, I love boats."
"Really? Why didn't you tell us before? Come with us next time!" said Jeff. "We were a bit bored yesterday. It's always just the three of us …"
"You were bored?" I asked. "But you looked so happy in the photos."
"Yeah," answered Jeff, "but everybody looks happy in the photos they post. We *have to* look happy, don't we? Sometimes it's hard work!"

Kate was right! Now I don't know why I felt so bad. Thanks Kate!

Lenny P.

1. Lenny felt bad when his friends had fun without him. *I felt sad*
2. Lenny wrote to Kate because of a photo. ______
3. Kate said that Lenny should talk to Jeff, Pam and Manisha. ______
4. Jeff invited Lenny to go to the boating lake with him and his friends. ______
5. Jeff is not always as happy as he looks in photos. ______
6. Lenny feels better now. ______

____ /5

WRITING

## 3 The new rule

*Read the information on the school noticeboard. Write an e-mail to Dave and tell him what the rule is, some things you can't do at school now and two reasons why you think the rule is good or bad.*

Think about phones at school. Make a list of reasons for and against them. Use those ideas for your e-mail.

**!!!!!! Important – Mobiles and smartphones at school !!!!!!**

Because students are using their phones too much in class and in the breaks, and because we have a problem with cyber bullies, we have made this new rule:

**You may bring your phone to school**

**BUT**

**you must turn it off for the whole school day!**

Dear Dave,

Our school has made a new rule about mobiles and smartphones.

______

______

______

______

______

______

______

______

______

______

____ /18

____ /29

# Class test 2

→ after Unit 5

LISTENING

## 1 When Dad was young …

8 ◎ *Listen to the conversation and complete the sentences. Use 1 to 3 words.*

1. Tim's dad is 50, but he doesn't feel ______________________.
2. Tim thinks that when his dad was a teenager, the world was very ______________________.
3. In the past Tim's father made plans with his friends when he saw them ______________________.
4. His dad didn't have a mobile, but he was able to call his friends ______________________.
5. Tim always calls his father when he's ______________________.
6. Tim is going to be his dad's first ______________________.

_____ /6

READING

## 2 A problem

*Read the two e-mails. Look at the statements on page 55 and write down the numbers of the lines which give you this information.*

**From:** Diana Stoppard

**To:** Amy McNeil | **Address book**

**Subject:** Louise

Dear Amy,

Thanks for posting that nice photo of us and for your message. Posts and e-mails are OK, but life was better when you lived here in Bradford!

I've got a problem now and I'm writing you an e-mail because I don't want other people to read this. Yesterday was Louise's birthday and … I forgot it! She was really angry. "Amy never forgot my birthday," she said. "When Amy was here, we three were good friends, but now I know: You only liked Amy. I can find better friends than you. Goodbye, Diana!"

I'm so upset. I've lost you and now I've lost Louise. What should I do?

Di xxx

**From:** Amy McNeil

**To:** Diana Stoppard | **Address book**

**Subject:** Re: Louise

Dear Di,

Oh no! First, you haven't lost me! We're still friends. But you have to talk to Louise. I think she was just angry for one moment. You could send her a nice card and write "Sorry, I forgot your birthday!" on it. Then invite her to do something fun with you. Buy cinema tickets, for example. But Di – you've forgotten my birthday before too, more than once! Here's my most important advice: Put your friends' birthdays in your phone!

See you in the summer holidays.

Love, Amy

| | line(s) |
|---|---|
| 1. Amy doesn't live in Bradford any more. | 3 |
| 2. Diana didn't write her problem as a comment on Amy's post. | |
| 3. Louise doesn't want to be friends with Diana now. | |
| 4. Amy thinks Diana and Louise should do something nice together. | |
| 5. Diana often forgets her friends' birthdays. | |

_____ /4

MEDIATION

## 3 The school's social network

*Your Welsh friend Jack asks you about social network rules at your school. Read the information on the school website and answer his questions in English.*

Aktuelles | Unsere Schule | Klassen | Aktivitäten | **Schulregeln** | Kontakt

Unsere Schule hat ein lebhaftes soziales Netzwerk im Internet. Dieses benutzen wir, um über Neuigkeiten zu informieren und über wichtige Schulereignisse zu berichten. Schüler und Lehrer haben zudem die Möglichkeit, über die Seite miteinander zu kommunizieren, soweit beide Parteien das möchten. Lehrer dürfen aber nicht davon ausgehen, dass alle Schüler das Netzwerk jederzeit benutzen können oder wollen. Deshalb ist es z. B. nicht erlaubt, Hausaufgaben über das Netzwerk zu geben. Außerdem dürfen hier keine Noten diskutiert und keine persönlichen oder beleidigenden Kommentare geschrieben werden. Die Lehrer erklären sich bereit, Fotos von sich auf der Seite zu erlauben. Fotos von Schülern dürfen nur mit ihrer ausdrücklichen Erlaubnis hochgeladen werden.

Persönliche soziale Netzwerke darf jeder nach Belieben benutzen. Wir raten jedoch davon ab, dass Lehrer und Schüler Online-Freunde werden. Nach Ende der Schulzeit bietet dies eine Möglichkeit in Kontakt zu bleiben – davor empfehlen wir, Online-Kontakte nur über die Schulseite zu pflegen.

Jack: What kind of things does your school post on its social network page?

You: ____________________________________________

Jack: Does everyone have to use it? And do the teachers use it to give you homework?

You: ____________________________________________

Jack: Can you post photos of teachers and students?

You: ____________________________________________

____________________________________________

Jack: What about your own social networks? Can you be online friends with your teachers?

You: ____________________________________________

____________________________________________

_____ /14

_____ /24

# Speaking

→ after Unit 1

PREPARE

## 1 Questions, questions

*Your friend was on holiday last month. Look at the words and write at least six questions about his or her holiday. Use the* ***simple past****.*

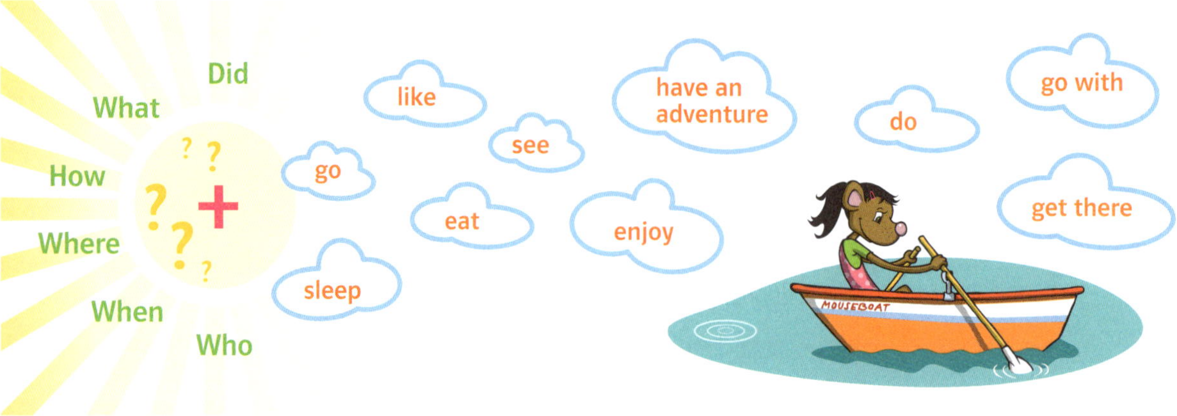


*Where did you go? Did you* ______________________________

______________________________

______________________________

______________________________

DIALOGUE

## 2 Where did you go on holiday?

*Make some notes about your last holiday. (The information can be true or not true.) Then ask and answer questions with a friend. Use the questions from exercise 1 and other questions.*

**Start:**

A: Hello Karen.
B: Hi Paul. Where did you go on your last holiday?
A: I went to the sea. And you, Karen? Where did you go?
B: I went to London!
A: Wow! What did you …?

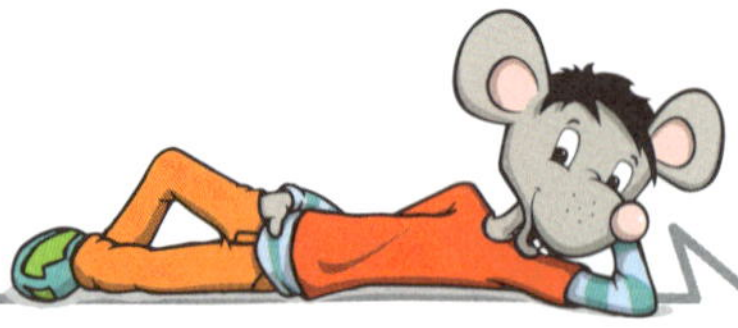

If possible, do exercise 2 with a friend from school. Then do exercise 3 with somebody in your family who speaks a little English (your mum / dad / older sister or brother / …).

MONOLOGUE

## 3 Is it true?

*Tell your partner about your friend's holiday. In the end your partner says "Yes, that's true." or "I don't think that's true."*

Karen went to London on her last holiday. She got there by train … .

# Speaking

→ after Unit 2

PREPARE

## 1 Subjects and activities at school

*Look at the school subjects and after-school activities. What do you think of them? Write them next to the headings and add two more subjects or activities.*

Art | Chess | Dance | Drama | Fashion Design | French | Film Studies | German | History | Humanities | Juggling | Maths | PE | Science | Technology

important: ______________________

______________________

fun: ______________________

important and fun: ______________________

______________________

MONOLOGUE

## 2 Talk about a subject or an activity

*Make a short presentation about a subject or an activity you want to have at your school. Use these ideas and take notes first. Then talk about the subject or activity for two minutes.*

*Subject:* ______________________

______________________

*Important because:* ______________________

______________________

______________________

*Fun because:* ______________________

______________________

______________________

*What you can learn:* ______________________

______________________

Hello! I want to talk about … . This is a really important subject / activity because … .

DIALOGUE

## 3 Choose a new subject

*Work with a partner and decide on a new subject for your school. Say why you find it important and what you can learn.*

I'd like to learn Drama in school.

That's fun but other subjects are more important.

Use comparative forms like "harder", "easier", "more interesting", "more fun" and "more important" to talk about different subjects.

# Speaking
→ after Unit 3

PREPARE

## 1 What do you know about London?

*Make notes under the three headings.*

| famous places | transport | activities |
| --- | --- | --- |
| *Buckingham Palace,* | | |

MONOLOGUE

## 2 What do you want to do in London?

*Look at the photos and talk about them for two minutes.*

The Science Museum

Madame Tussauds

Answer these questions:
- What can you see in the photos?
- What can you do there?
- Do you want to go there? Why, or why not?

DIALOGUE

## 3 How do I get to . . .?

*Use the information below and the map of the Tube at the back of your book. Act out the two role plays with a partner. You are at South Kensington station.*

Partner A: *You are a tourist.*
- Ask your partner how to get to Oxford Circus.
- You didn't really understand. Ask him / her to explain it again.
- Say thank you and goodbye.

Partner B: *You are a Londoner.*
- Describe to your partner how he / she can get where he / she wants to go.
- Answer your partner.

Partner A: *Now you are a Londoner.*
- Describe to your partner how to get where he / she wants to go.
- Answer your partner.

Partner B: *Now you are a tourist.*
- Ask your partner how to get to Lancaster Gate.
- You didn't really understand. Ask him / her to explain it again.
- Say thank you and goodbye.

# Speaking

→ after Unit 4

PREPARE

## 1 Sports injuries

*Think of health problems which could come from doing a sport. Make a mind map.*

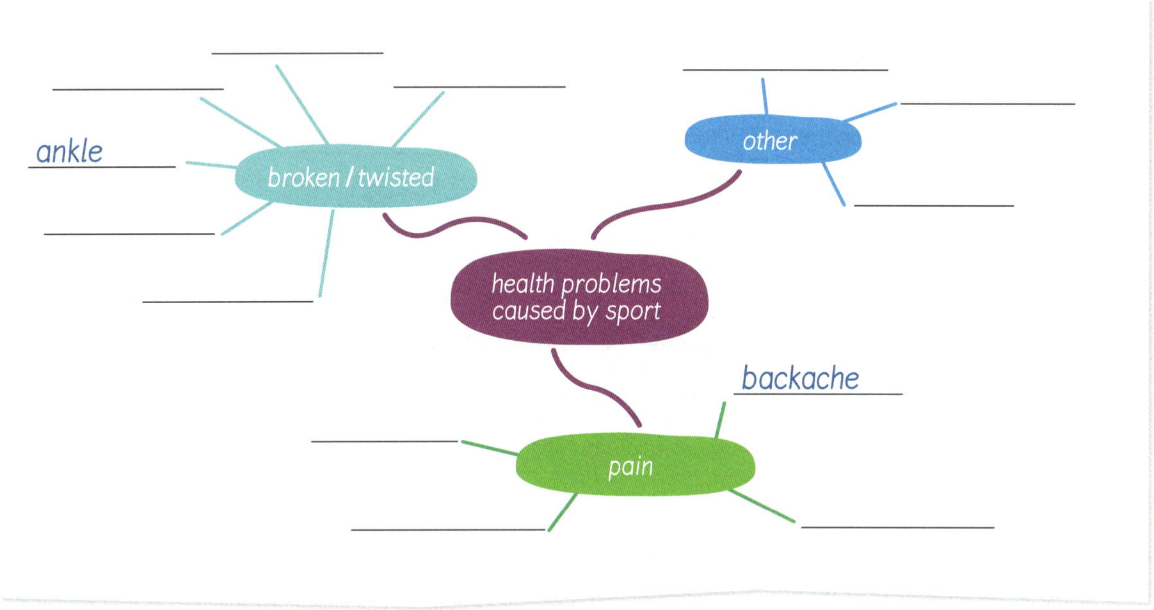


DIALOGUE

## 2 An interview with a doctor

**a)** *Use the information and prepare your role. Take notes on a separate piece of paper.*

Partner A: *You are a reporter and you interview a doctor after a marathon.*

Prepare questions about …
- problems and injuries people had.
- mistakes people make when they run.
- tips the doctor has for runners.

Partner B: *You are a doctor who was helping at a marathon.*

Make notes about …
- problems and injuries people had.
- mistakes people make when they run.
- tips you have for runners.

**b)** *Act out the interview. Then take turns.*

**Start:**

A: Hello Doctor Walker. Can I ask you a few questions about marathons and health?

B: Yes, of course.

MONOLOGUE

## 3 A radio report

*Use your notes in exercise 2 a) and prepare a radio report. Talk about injuries and health problems at the marathon yesterday and the doctor's advice for runners.*

Welcome to this week's programme "Healthy and happy." Yesterday was marathon day … .

# Speaking

→ after Unit 5

PREPARE

## 1 Good or bad advice?

**a)** *Here are some things people have said about the best way to use social networks. Do you think the advice is good or bad? Write 'G' for good advice and 'B' for bad advice.*

| | |
|---|---|
| 1. You should never post photos of yourself. | |
| 2. Don't let everyone see your home address. | |
| 3. Only become "friends" with people you have met face-to-face. | |
| 4. You should write nasty comments when you don't like a post. | |
| 5. You should share all your problems online. | |
| 6. Never become online "friends" with your parents. | |
| 7. Always use your real name online. | |
| 8. Block people who make you feel bad. | |
| 9. Don't let friends post photos of you. | |
| 10. Don't believe everything you see online. | |

**b)** *Make notes for three more tips.*

______________________________

______________________________

MONOLOGUE

## 2 It's good advice *sometimes* ...

*Choose one tip from exercise 1 that you think is good advice* ***sometimes but not always****. Talk about it for two minutes.*

I want to talk about posting photos of friends. Sometimes I'm angry when friends post photos of me that I don't like.

Answer these questions:
- What is the advice?
- When is it good advice?
- Why is not always good advice?
- In which situations could it be difficult to follow the advice?
- How could you change the advice and make it better?

DIALOGUE

## 3 Our class page

*Your class is creating a profile for a new social network site called Classbook. Decide with your partner what information should be on the profile and find three rules for how to use the page.*

**Start:** A: What about a photo of the whole class for our profile picture?
B: No, we can't do that because ... .

**Useful phrases**

What about ... ? | What do you ... ? | Can we ... ? | We can't do that because ... . | We can / want to / ... . | That's a good idea. | But we must / mustn't ... . | I agree. | So, our three rules are ... .

# Summer holidays

*Write a blog entry about your summer holidays. Think of a special moment or experience and describe what happened. Say where you were, who was with you, what you did and how you felt. Add a photo or a picture, if you want to.*

## My holiday blog

# Irregular verbs

■ ■ ■ Grundform, *simple past* und *past participle* sind identisch
■ ● ● Grundform unterscheidet sich vom *simple past* und *past participle*
■ ● ■ Grundform und *past participle* sind identisch, nur das *simple past* hat eine andere Form
■ ● ▲ Grundform, *simple past* und *past participle* haben alle eine andere Form

| ■ Grundform | ■ simple past | ■ past participle | Deutsch |
|---|---|---|---|
| cost [kɒst] | cost [kɒst] | cost [kɒst] | kosten |
| cut [kʌt] | cut [kʌt] | cut [kʌt] | schneiden |
| hit [hɪt] | hit [hɪt] | hit [hɪt] | schlagen, treffen |
| hurt [hɜːt] | hurt [hɜːt] | hurt [hɜːt] | verletzen, sich weh tun |
| let [let] | let [let] | let [let] | lassen |
| put [pʊt] | put [pʊt] | put [pʊt] | legen, setzen, stellen |
| set up ['set ˌʌp] | set up ['set ˌʌp] | set up ['set ˌʌp] | erbauen, errichten |

| ■ Grundform | ● simple past | ● past participle | Deutsch |
|---|---|---|---|
| bring [brɪŋ] | brought [brɔːt] | brought [brɔːt] | (mit)bringen |
| build [bɪld] | built [bɪlt] | built [bɪlt] | bauen |
| buy [baɪ] | bought [bɔːt] | bought [bɔːt] | kaufen |
| feel [fiːl] | felt [felt] | felt [felt] | fühlen |
| find [faɪnd] | found [faʊnd] | found [faʊnd] | finden |
| get [get] | got [gɒt] | got [gɒt] | bekommen, erhalten |
| have [hæv] | had [hæd] | had [hæd] | haben |
| hear [hɪə] | heard [hɜːd] | heard [hɜːd] | hören |
| hold [həʊld] | held [held] | held [held] | halten |
| keep [kiːp] | kept [kept] | kept [kept] | (auf)bewahren, behalten |
| learn [lɜːn] | learned [lɜːnd]<br>learnt [lɜːnt] | learned [lɜːnd]<br>learnt [lɜːnt] | lernen |
| leave [liːv] | left [left] | left [left] | (ver)lassen |
| make [meɪk] | made [meɪd] | made [meɪd] | machen, tun |
| meet [miːt] | met [met] | met [met] | treffen |
| pay [peɪ] | paid [peɪd] | paid [peɪd] | (be)zahlen |
| read [riːd] | read [red] | read [red] | lesen |
| retell [ˌriː'tel] | retold [ˌriː'təʊld] | retold [ˌriː'təʊld] | nacherzählen |
| say [seɪ] | said [sed] | said [sed] | sagen |
| sell [sel] | sold [səʊld] | sold [səʊld] | verkaufen |
| send [send] | sent [sent] | sent [sent] | senden, verschicken |
| sit [sɪt] | sat [sæt] | sat [sæt] | sitzen |
| sleep [sliːp] | slept [slept] | slept [slept] | schlafen |
| spell [spel] | spelt [spelt] | spelt [spelt] | buchstabieren |

| | | | |
|---|---|---|---|
| spend [spend] | spent [spent] | spent [spent] | ausgeben, verbringen |
| stand (up) [stænd] | stood (up) [stʊd] | stood (up) [stʊd] | (auf)stehen |
| tell [tel] | told [təʊld] | told [təʊld] | erzählen |
| think [θɪŋk] | thought [θɔ:t] | thought [θɔ:t] | (nach)denken, glauben |
| understand [ˌʌndə'stænd] | understood [ˌʌndə'stʊd] | understood [ˌʌndə'stʊd] | verstehen |
| win [wɪn] | won [wʌn] | won [wʌn] | gewinnen, siegen |

| ■ Grundform | ● simple past | ■ past participle | Deutsch |
|---|---|---|---|
| become [bɪ'kʌm] | became [bɪ'keɪm] | become [bɪ'kʌm] | werden |
| come [kʌm] | came [keɪm] | come [kʌm] | kommen |
| run [rʌn] | ran [ræn] | run [rʌn] | laufen, rennen |

| ■ Grundform | ● simple past | ▲ past participle | Deutsch |
|---|---|---|---|
| be [bi:] | was / were [wɒz / wɜ:] | been [bi:n] | sein |
| blow (out) [bləʊ] | blew [blu:] | blown [bləʊn] | (aus)blasen, (aus)pusten |
| break [breɪk] | broke [brəʊk] | broken ['brəʊkn] | (zer)brechen, kaputt machen |
| choose [tʃu:z] | chose [tʃəʊz] | chosen ['tʃəʊzn] | (aus)wählen |
| do [du:] | did [dɪd] | done [dʌn] | machen, tun |
| draw [drɔ:] | drew [dru:] | drawn [drɔ:n] | zeichnen |
| drink [drɪŋk] | drank [dræŋk] | drunk [drʌŋk] | trinken |
| eat [i:t] | ate [et] | eaten ['i:tn] | essen |
| fall [fɔ:l] | fell [fel] | fallen ['fɔ:lən] | fallen |
| fly [flaɪ] | flew [flu:] | flown [fləʊn] | fliegen |
| forget [fə'get] | forgot [fə'gɒt] | forgotten [fə'gɒtn] | vergessen |
| give [gɪv] | gave [geɪv] | given['gɪvn] | geben |
| go [gəʊ] | went [went] | gone [gɒn] | gehen, fahren |
| know [nəʊ] | knew [nju:] | known [nəʊn] | kennen, wissen |
| see [si:] | saw [sɔ:] | seen [si:n] | sehen |
| show [ʃəʊ] | showed [ʃəʊd] | shown [ʃəʊn] | zeigen |
| sing [sɪŋ] | sang [sæŋ] | sung [sʌŋ] | singen |
| speak [spi:k] | spoke [spəʊk] | spoken ['spəʊkn] | sprechen |
| swim [swɪm] | swam [swæm] | swum [swʌm] | schwimmen |
| take [teɪk] | took [tʊk] | taken ['teɪkn] | nehmen |
| throw [θrəʊ] | threw [θru:] | thrown [θrəʊn] | werfen |
| wear [weə] | wore [wɔ:] | worn [wɔ:n] | anhaben, tragen |
| write [raɪt] | wrote [rəʊt] | written ['rɪtn] | schreiben |

## Hörverstehenstexte

| Track | Unit | Test, Exercise | Title | Time |
|---|---|---|---|---|
| 1 | 1 | Class test 1, exercise 1 | After the trip to Wales | 02:11 |
| 2 | 1 | Class test 2, exercise 1 | A bed in a tree | 01:28 |
| 3 | 2 | Class test 1, exercise 1 | Lisa and Diana talk about films | 02:02 |
| 4 | 2 | Class test 2, exercise 1 | The Cooking Club | 01:36 |
| 5 | 3 | Class test 2, exercise 1 | Where do they want to go? | 03:01 |
| 6 | 4 | Class test 1, exercise 1 | At the stadium | 01:49 |
| 7 | 4 | Class test 2, exercise 1 | At the doctor's | 02:03 |
| 8 | 5 | Class test 2, exercise 1 | When Dad was young … | 02:11 |

Gesamtspielzeit: 16:43

## Filme

| Unit | Test, Exercise | Title | Time |
|---|---|---|---|
| 3 | Class test 1, exercise 1 | London life | 01:38 |
| 5 | Class test 1, exercise 1 | In the news | 00:40 |

Gesamtspielzeit: 02:18

Außerdem findest du auf dieser CD-ROM:
- alle Transkripte zu den Hörverstehenstexten.
- die Skripte zu den beiden Filmen.
- das Lösungsheft.

**Systemvoraussetzungen der CD-ROM**
- Webbrowser ab:
  Microsoft Internet Explorer 5.5, Mozilla Firefox 2.0, Safari 3.0, Opera 9.0, Konqueror 3.2
- 512 MB RAM
- CD-ROM Laufwerk
- Adobe Reader ab Version 5
- Adobe Flash Player ab Version 9
- Medienplayer für mp3-Dateien

**Hinweis:** Bei der eingelegten CD handelt es sich um eine Multisession-CD.
Die darauf ebenfalls vorhandenen Audio-Dateien werden Ihnen am PC im Normalfall nicht angezeigt. Sie können nur auf einem CD-Spieler angehört werden.

Sollten Sie Probleme mit dem vorliegenden Programm haben, finden Sie in der Datei „Hotline.txt“, die sich auf der obersten Ebene der CD-ROM befindet, unsere Kontaktdaten und weitere Hilfestellungen.

Auf der CD-ROM befindet sich ein ausführliches Handbuch zum Programm.